THE
RULES
TO
BREAK

RICHARD TEMPLAR

Harlow, England • London • New York • Boston • San Francisco • Toronto • Sydney
Auckland • Singapore • Hong Kong • Tokyo • Seoul • Taipei • New Delhi
Cape Town • São Paulo • Mexico City • Madrid • Amsterdam • Munich • Paris • Milan

PEARSON EDUCATION LIMITED
Edinburgh Gate
Harlow CM20 2JE
United Kingdom
Tel: +44 (0)1279 623623
Web: www.pearson.com/uk

First published 2013 (print and electronic)
Second edition published 2014 (print and electronic)
This edition published 2016 (print and electronic)

ISBN: 978-1-292-08812-9 (print)
       978-1-292-08814-3 (PDF)
       978-1-292-08815-0 (ePub)
       978-1-292-08813-6 (eText)

British Library Cataloguing-in-Publication Data
A catalogue record for the print edition is available from the British Library

Library of Congress Cataloging-in-Publication Data
A catalog record for the print edition is available from the Library of Congress

10 9 8 7 6 5 4 3
19 18 17 16

Cover design by Nick Redeyoff

Print edition typeset in 10.5/12pt ITC Berkeley Oldstyle Std by 71
Print edition printed and bound in Great Britain by Clays Ltd, Bungay, Suffolk

NOTE THAT ANY PAGE CROSS REFERENCES REFER TO THE PRINT EDITION

Contents

Rules to follow 204

Introduction

When you're young you're told all sorts of things: I want doesn't get, the best things in life are free, familiarity breeds contempt, patience is a virtue. And others personal to your own family or teachers. Some of them are drilled into you, some of them you just pick up along the way. As you get older, you pick up even more sayings, principles and beliefs, many of which you just assume to be true and never think to question. So by the time you arrive into adulthood, you're living by a mixed bag of so-called 'rules', whether you know it or not. You might only know it when you suddenly find yourself spouting one of them to a struggling friend or youngster and then think 'Where on earth did that come from?'

Trouble is, these principles, given as 'advice' from well-meaning people, often aren't true. And many of them are right some of the time, but whoever told them to you failed to explain that there will be times when you should disregard them, or even take the opposite approach.

The point is, you have to learn to question, to think for yourself, not to follow mindlessly the rules set down for you by other people. Otherwise you'll be making yourself miserable for no reason. Learn to trust your own judgement (now there's a proverb you can follow all the time).

I'm not saying everything you're taught is wrong, whether it's a popular homily or a value impressed on you by your family. I'd entirely agree, for example, that it's always a good idea to look before you leap. But I agree with it after having thought it through. However, I also think, for example, that it can sometimes be a very good idea to change horses in midstream. And I disagree that attack is the best form of defence, although once in a while it may be the only one that works. And money is certainly not the root of all evil. We can't pass the blame on to those poor, inanimate notes and coins.

These pretender rules may not all be popular sayings, however. Some of them are beliefs that are incredibly widespread among people. They may be worded in any one of a dozen different ways, but boiled down they all mean the same thing, and the underlying common theme is seriously unhelpful.

Since writing *The Rules of Life* and my other Rules books (which outline the behaviours of people who get the most out of life and find it easiest and most fulfilling), I've discovered that people really do love rules. And that's part of the problem. Many of us love rules to the point that we just don't think to question them. I've had a lot of emails from readers who have discovered that they are living by rules that are actually what I'd call 'imposters' – well-meant advice or beliefs they have just picked up along the way. And that's why I set out to write this book. To shine a light on the unhelpful beliefs and behaviours that so many of us are carrying around and give them a good poke to see if they really do pass muster.

Think. That's the message. Question everything you've been taught, and don't live by other people's rules* until you've considered whether you agree with them. Whether you're 18 or 80, examine the childhood strictures you were told to follow blindly, and decide for yourself whether they're right. Just regularly catch yourself and ask 'Why do I believe that?' and 'Is it helpful?'

I'm not giving you permission to ignore any rules and values you don't happen to like. (I wouldn't do that – you don't need my permission for anything.) That's not the way to happiness or success. Be honest with yourself, and sometimes you'll find yourself reluctantly agreeing with principles you wish you didn't. Just don't get tied down unthinkingly to other people's values. When you become an adult you're allowed to develop your own set of principles.

---

* Yep, even mine.

So here are the so-called rules that I encourage you to break, at least some of the time. These are the ones I've found to be surprisingly common among people from all walks of life. At the end of each entry, I offer you a more reliable 'replacement' or proper Rule to put in its place. I hope you find them useful, and do let me know how you get on. You can contact me via my Facebook page, www.facebook.com/richardtemplar. I can't promise always to find time to respond, but I can promise you that I'll read your post with interest, and I'd love to know about any rules you've successfully broken.

Richard Templar

Acknowledgements

I would like to thank the many people who have helped me with this book, and especially the following readers:

Olabisi Adebule
Nikki Betts
Ned Craze
Glendon Hall
Virginia Josey
Debra Pennington-Bick
Nick Saunders

Publisher's acknowledgements

We are grateful to the following for permission to reproduce copyright material:

Poem on page 93, 'The Middle' from *Candy is Dandy: The best of Ogden Nash*, Andre Deutsch Limited (Smith, L. and Eberstadt, I. (editors) 1994). Reprinted by permission of Carlton Books Ltd and Copyright © 1949 by Ogden Nash, renewed. Reprinted by permission of Curtis Brown, Ltd.

In some instances we have been unable to trace the owners of copyright material, and we would appreciate any information that would enable us to do so.

RULES
TO BREAK

"Success is a good job earning lots of money"

People are always ready to tell you that you'll never be successful if you don't do this or that. I'm willing to bet that you've already heard something like: 'You'll never make anything of your life unless you knuckle down and work harder/go to university/pass your exams/get a well-paid job/get a "proper" job.' You know the kind of thing.

But hang on. How are we defining success? And is there only one narrow path that leads there?

The parents, teachers or well-intentioned friends who tell you these things are probably assuming what you want out of life is a nice house and plenty of money and a job that commands respect.

Let's set aside for a minute whether they're right about that, and assume it is for now. Is it really true that being good at exams, going to university, landing a job at a prestigious firm and working your way up the corporate ladder is the only way to achieve those material goals? No, of course not. It's one way, but not the only way. There are plenty of real people who've left school early and made a fortune.

But who says that money and an important job *are* the things that constitute success for you? They may be commonly used measures of success, but that doesn't make them right.

The only way to determine what makes for success is to establish what will make you content with your life. And for some people that might mean a flashy car or an impressive job title. If that does it for you, fine, then that's the thing to aim for.

But if it just doesn't feel right, that's because you're one of the many people who are looking for something else in life. Success to you could mean a big family with lots of kids, or a job that leaves you enough time to pursue your other interests, or the satisfaction that you're helping people, or an absorbing job that fascinates you even if the pay is rubbish and the promotion prospects zero.

I know someone who only felt content that he'd achieved what he wanted when he was living self-sufficiently on a wild Welsh hillside with just his dog for company. And someone else who only felt successful when she was able to get a flat in London and live the city life, regardless of the fact that her job was pretty basic and going nowhere. I know people who've regarded success as being able to get out of the big city and live quietly in the country with a more modest job and a smaller house. And those who have been happy in almost any job so long as it keeps them out of doors. One of my sons is really happy living on a classic boat he's spent years restoring – he's not bothered about how he earns the money to look after the boat. His feeling of success comes from having rescued it and created his own home from it.

Even the people who do hanker after a more traditional idea of success can have widely differing views of it. Some want money to flash it around, others so they feel safe. Some people want a top job for the status, others for the challenge. We're all different. For almost everyone, attaining success will mean hard work and a clear focus. But only you can know what to focus on.

So don't let anyone tell you what it takes to succeed, because they have no idea what success means to you. You, on the other hand, need to think about what it means, or you can't work towards it.

RULE 1

Success is what you say it is

"Some people are just born lucky"

It's easy to want someone else's life, to covet what they've got, to wish you had their skills, talents, friends, money, lifestyle. That's because you can only see what's on the surface – what they let you see. And you probably only notice the stuff that you envy.

When I was a lad, there was this kid in our class who did brilliantly in every subject. He was so brainy he barely had to try. Boy, did I wish I could be like him. It was several years before I realized that actually he worked a lot harder than I thought. He was bright, but not that exceptional. And the reason he worked hard was because his parents were strict disciplinarians and wouldn't let him watch TV or go out unless he'd done the work they expected from him. With hindsight, I was glad no one had listened to my younger self and waved a magic wand and given me his life. I'd have hated it.

Actually, thinking about it, there were kids at school going through all kinds of stuff we knew nothing about at the time. Alcoholism, bereavement, divorce, abuse . . . and it's still true as an adult that I probably don't know the half of what goes on in other people's lives.

So I've stopped envying people, because I have no idea whether I really want to be them or not. At least I know where I am, being me. I'm used to it, and I have some control over it too, which counts for a lot. And even if other people seem genuinely happy and well-off now, who's to say where they're headed? It could all come crashing down in a few years, and I'll be very relieved I stuck with being me.

Besides, have you ever stopped to think about the people who envy you? I bet there are a few. Maybe they envy the whole 'you' thing, or perhaps it's something specific – your confidence, your skill with a football, your friends, your party invitations, your university degree. We have a daft tendency to take for granted the things we have, and just focus on what we lack. Maybe we should see ourselves through other people's eyes more often. We're all a mishmash of positives and negatives, and your own mix is no better or worse than anyone else's.

And there's another thing. As long as you focus on other people, you don't get round to tackling the things you dislike about your own life. Instead of wishing you had what they have, why not spend a bit more time thinking about how to get what you want for yourself? A bit less self-pity and a bit more get-up-and-go and there'd be nothing to envy.

> # RULE 2
> # Don't envy other people

"You need the right qualifications"

Sweating over coursework? Under pressure to get the best grades you can? Teachers or parents or friends or tutors telling you how your whole future depends on it? Let me tell you a secret – exam results really aren't as important as everyone tells you.

They're a shortcut. That's all. A good exam grade tells a university or an employer what they need to know in the simplest way. But plenty of people have happy and successful lives on the back of some pretty rubbish exam results. Einstein famously failed his university entrance exam, proving that there's also a lot exam results don't say about you.

Look, I'm not saying don't bother. For most people, life is a lot easier if they get the best grades they can. Plus if you're young it certainly smoothes your relationship with your parents. But it's not worth making yourself miserable over. You can retake exams, go back to college 5 or 25 years later, work your way up from the bottom, pick a career that doesn't need qualifications . . . So long as you have dedication and aren't afraid of hard work, you can do most things with or without good exam grades.

I'll tell you something: since 2 years after I left school, not one employer has ever asked me what grades (if any) I got. OK, that wouldn't happen in any career, but there are still countless jobs where experience and natural ability count for far more than exams. When you're 18, they're all an employer has to go on. By the time you're 28, they're far more interested in what you've done with the last 10 years of your life than what you did at school.

And another thing – I remember all that sweating over whether to take chemistry or physics, or which language option to do, or whether we really needed to take history. But unless you're going into a very specific career such as medicine, I can tell you it just doesn't matter what subjects you take. Take the ones you'll enjoy.

Do you know, my commissioning editor for this book has a degree in physics. What damn use is that for a career in publishing? Bet she sweated buckets over choosing it when she was 18 though. I know a comedy writer who studied ancient Greek. I have a brother-in-law who agonized over whether to do philosophy or computing – not knowing then that he'd work in conservation, for which he'd actually want a degree in environmental biology. So he went back 5 years later and got one of those too.

You see? Everyone else just wants the best for you and all that stuff, and they feel safer if you get top grades, but the truth is that you may not need any of it – and if you do need something you don't get, you can sort it out later. What appears to matter desperately now will seem like a fuss about nothing in a few years' time.

RULE 3

Exams aren't the be all and end all

"Your parents are always right"

Here's something that should be aimed at young people – but I have a sneaky feeling that lots of us go on needing to refer to it for a long time after we've left home.

When we're young we assume (unless there are very strong reasons to the contrary) that our parents are perfect. We may not like the rules and boundaries they set, but we figure they must be right. As we move into our teens, we start to notice that some of our friends' parents are really quite different from our own. But there's still an underlying feeling that ours are probably the ones who've got it right.

Think about it. From as far back as you can remember, your parents have been practising being parents. They've had a lifetime (yours) to plan and hone and fine-tune what they're doing. So surely they must be pretty near perfect by now. Why wouldn't they be?

Look, take it from me – as a parent six times over – that no parent is ever perfect. Apart from the fact that the job is so difficult, we carry so much baggage along, from the way we were brought up by our own parents, to our values, our hopes, our own experiences, our anxieties . . . everything we've ever done or feared or thought feeds into the way we treat our kids.

On top of that, every child is different. Even if your mum or dad felt confident about how to treat your brother or sister, that doesn't mean they know how to cope with you. Some children push all the boundaries, some are worriers, some work too hard, some struggle to make friends, some are big risk-takers, some give up easily. Some are just like yourself, and others are so different you have no idea what makes them tick. I remember my eldest child challenging me at one point, telling me I should know what to do because I'd been a parent for 14 years (at the time). I pointed out that I'd never been the parent of a 14-year-old before, so I didn't have enough relevant experience to draw on.

See? The bottom line is that your parents are making it up as they go along. Honestly. Some parents are very good at thinking on their feet, but they're still making the whole thing up. I should know – I've been doing it for years.*

All of this means that you should listen to your parents, but don't be afraid to make your own decisions once you're old enough – whether that's 15 or 50 is up to you. Your parents are doing their best, but once you hit adulthood, you don't have to follow their advice any more. Listen politely, of course, but you're in charge now. They'll often be right, but not always.

RULE 4
Don't expect your parents to be perfect

---

* Obviously you must *never* tell my kids this. I'm trusting you here . . .

"Your parents are responsible for how you turn out"

Having established that your parents aren't perfect – can't possibly be perfect – it stands to reason that you can't really blame them when they get things wrong. They're doing their best.

Suppose someone told you that you had to – let's say – run the national railway network.* No training. Just thrown in at the deep end. Do you reckon you'd get it right first time? Of course not. So why expect your mum and dad to get it right when they're suddenly plunged into dealing with you? By the time they've got the hang of coping with babies, you've morphed into a toddler. Once they're getting on top of that, you're off to school. When that seems to be going OK, suddenly you're turning into a teenager, which is a whole new parenting thing again.

What's more, although you may have been only dimly aware of this growing up, they'll also have been coping with their work, your siblings, their parents, family crises, money worries and all the rest of it. So, thinking about it, it's not very reasonable to blame them for every mistake they made.

The thing about being a parent is that you don't get a dummy run at it to find out if you're suited. Babysitting other people's children just doesn't come close. So by the time you get a chance to see if you're any good at it, you're already committed. If it turns out not to be your thing, there's sod all you can do about it. Of course most parents do a decent enough job despite this, but none of us gets it right all the time.

---

* If you're in a country like Iceland that has no national railway network you'll just have to think of an equivalent.

The important thing is to consider your parents' intentions. If they're doing the best job they can, if they have your interests at heart, if they love you, then you'll have to settle for that. It's more than some people get. As one parenting expert said, 'As a parent, your job is simply to keep them alive until they can get help'. And as we saw in the last Rule, once you're an adult, you don't have to do what they say any more.

I do just want to say that there are some things you *can* blame your parents for, if you're unlucky enough to have been on the receiving end. If your parents have treated you in ways that are against the law – physical, verbal, sexual or psychological abuse, criminal neglect – then you can blame them. Even so, if you can get to a place where you can nevertheless forgive them, try to do so. Not because they deserve it, but because you do.

RULE 5
Give your parents a break

"The world is against you"

Listen, we all get good breaks and bad breaks. People treat us badly, or we get lucky and they spoil us. We all have great teachers, rubbish friends, tricky mums or dads, difficult siblings, supportive adults when we're growing up . . . a whole mishmash of influences. Sure, on balance some of us get luckier than others, but we all have negative stuff to contend with. And positive stuff to contend with too.

Once you've left home, however, it's down to you – whoever you are. You can't go around blaming other people for all the bits of your life that aren't how you'd like them to be. It's not your parents' fault, or your school's, or anyone else's. Maybe it was, when you were a little kid, but not any more.

I'm not being unsympathetic. I'm not saying I don't care. I'm just saying that this is how it is. No one else but you can make the rest of your life better. It's no good blaming other people for messing up your childhood, and then going ahead and messing up your own adulthood. If you can't make a decent job of your life yourself, why do you think anyone else should have been able to?

Sometimes blaming other people is the easy option. And yes, maybe you deserve an easy option after what you've been through. But not half as much as you deserve a good life from now on. And that can't happen as long as you put responsibility for your current happiness on the shoulders of your past. You need to wrest control of your life from all of those people who mishandled your childhood, and show them how it *should* be done.

Of course, this means that when you make bad decisions or poor judgements or unethical choices, that's down to you. But, if you're a true Rules player, that won't happen often. When it does, you'll stand up and admit to it – just like all those people who influenced your childhood should have done. Maybe some of them did. You won't blame anyone else, because your life from now on is down to you – the good and the bad.

This isn't just about what's right and fair, it's about what works for you. Have you ever noticed how the people who accept responsibility for themselves are happier? They don't feel out of control, victims of circumstance. Sure, not everything is under our control, and things will go against us from time to time, but if we're in charge, we can take action to put them right – or at least to deal with the aftermath in our own way.

If you blame other people, or events, you're turning yourself into a victim when you could be a winner. The world is full of people who prove this point – if you think about it you'll know plenty of people who have had tough lives but refuse to see themselves as victims, from icons like Nelson Mandela, to some of your own friends. Why wouldn't you want to join them?

RULE 6
You're responsible for your own life

"We all have an absolute right to be respected"

My children like to wind each other up – at least when they're feeling frustrated or under the weather or tired. It's what siblings do. Many years ago, we foolishly made it a 'rule' at home that they weren't allowed to do this. If they knew that what they were doing was frustrating one of their siblings, they were to stop. Now, that might seem reasonable to you – it did to me – but of course kids have an irritating habit of subverting rules.

It wasn't long before I'd overhear them saying to each other, 'Stop whistling, it's winding me up. You're not allowed to wind me up'. Or 'It really irritates me when you leave the knife in the butter. If you know it irritates me, you're not allowed to do it'. Yep, that's right, they'd taken our rule and metaphorically scribbled all over it and then jumped up and down on it.* Now we found ourselves making another rule to qualify the first one: you have to be tolerant.

Of course it's impossible to stop siblings quarrelling, and indeed you shouldn't try to. It's good for them. But they do like things to be black and white, and this just isn't. The fact is that we do all have a right to be treated with respect, but we also have to temper that with tolerance of other people. Otherwise the whole of life becomes a series of arguments with neighbours, colleagues, authorities, friends and family.

Yes, I know your neighbour should have checked with you before pruning their side of your tree. But how much does it

---

* I tried in vain pointing out to them that this really wound me up, so therefore they should stop doing it.

really matter? OK, so your flatmate never remembers to replace the coffee when it runs out. But come on – they're great company and they keep the place clean and tidy. You can't have everything. Would it hurt so much to replace the coffee yourself?

It can help to put yourself in other people's shoes here. Are they genuinely doing this irritating thing out of disrespect for you – in which case you have every right to challenge it (diplomatically, I hope) – or are they just being themselves? Do they simply have different priorities or preoccupations to you? Maybe they're being thoughtless, but that's still a long way from deliberate disrespect.

And while you're putting yourself in other people's shoes, think about how you come across to other people. Is it possible that you have any teensy weensy annoying habits? Might you ever irritate other people at all, do you think? Not out of disrespect for them, but just out of seeing the world from your own perspective? We all do it, so perhaps we should be a little more forgiving and tolerant when other people do it to us. Unless they're our brother or sister of course. Then it's everyone for themselves, apparently.

RULE 7
There's a balance between the right to respect, and tolerance

---

"You can choose your friends but you can't choose your family"

Surely this one is unarguably true? Well, unfortunately it's one of those throwaway lines that can be really damaging and leave you short-changed in life. Of course you can't choose your family in the literal sense. But in the majority of cases you *can* choose to make them your friends. Even though it can take some effort, it's well worth it. Any psychologist will tell you that siblings grow up in competition with each other. In particular, they compete for their parents' attention. And they work hard to make themselves different, so that they'll attract individual notice. It's a deep evolutionary drive that we're unaware of, especially as children.

In some families it can drive a wedge between brothers and sisters. Which is somewhat unfair, since all that's happening is that kids too young to know any better are just following their basic instincts. Some parents manage to respond as fairly as they can, but others struggle to manage the competition, or even seem to encourage the rivalry.

Once we've grown up and left home, we need to put all that behind us. Oh, I know that's harder than it sounds, and we may not always succeed, but we need to keep working at it.

Why? Because our siblings will be with us for longer than anyone else. When our parents are gone, our brothers and sisters will have been around for longer than anyone else. They know what we're really like – the bits we're ashamed of, the bits we've hidden from the rest of the world, the bits we'd rather forget. So when we need a friend, they'll be there, with a stronger bond than anyone else.

I know two brothers who fought as kids, like most brothers do. They played together too, of course. But somehow they carried their childhood squabbles into adulthood, and by their late twenties they barely spoke to each other. Then their dad died suddenly, and somehow, as the family came together, the two of them found that their strongest support came from each other. Since then they've been best of mates. They've learnt what old behaviours to avoid, and retrained themselves in some areas of their relationship, and they've rediscovered the friendship they had as children.

You have to work out what childhood patterns your relationship is falling into, and then work to change them. One friend of mine was asked – very pleasantly – by her younger brother to stop treating him like a kid. She took this on board, and next time he came to stay she bit her lip a few times. And interestingly she noticed that when she stopped bossing him around, he kept asking what to do about this or that – all things most people would work out for themselves. So she decided to have another chat with him, and explained that if she was going to stop bossing him around, he'd have to stop behaving like a child. He took the point, and she tells me they now have a much better, and more equal, relationship.

So if your sister is still trying to steal your friends, or your brother hasn't stopped competing with you (even if it's money or job titles these days, instead of sport or school grades), you need to make changes to break the pattern. Don't assume it's all their fault – it's not. It's no one's fault. It's just how families are. But we all need to evolve as we get older. Otherwise the next time we really need a friend who understands us, we'll have deprived ourselves of the best friend of all.

RULE 8
Your siblings should be your best friends for life

"Teacher knows best"

When I left school at 16, my head teacher told me I'd never amount to anything. Well, I haven't saved the world, or become Prime Minister, but I feel I've done OK.

The trouble with most teachers is that they know very little about anything but teaching. Many of them are married to people in similar professions. They work in institutions all their lives. Theirs is a narrow world.

They do an invaluable job, mind you. The best teachers can be a positive influence on hundreds of kids, and can inspire them to lifelong achievement. I'm not dissing them – as teachers. But I know very few teachers who have any idea what is entailed in, say, being an airline pilot, or working for an international development charity, or setting up your own business.* Why should they? The best teachers readily acknowledge this.

So most of the time they're on solid ground teaching you the exam syllabus, and hopefully enthusing you about the subject. But beyond that, don't take what they say too much to heart. I've known children berated endlessly for poor handwriting, for example, without ever being reassured that in most jobs it won't matter in the least. They'll be using a computer anyway. We'd all prefer good handwriting, but if it eludes you it doesn't matter nearly as much as your teachers will make out.

Some teachers bang on about the need to conform. And lots of us don't have a problem with that. But some people do. If you're a teacher, it's true that you do need to conform, as you work in an institution that relies heavily on it. And that's where some teachers fail to see beyond their own world. The fact is, if you want to be a research scientist, or a graphic designer, or a freelance

---

* And that covers most of the Business Studies teachers I've met, by the way.

writer, there will be lots of opportunities for you where your non-conformist outlook will be accepted or even embraced.

So remember that teachers don't know everything. They know a great deal about their own subject, about learning, about working in a traditional institution, about children. But there are big gaps in their knowledge of the world too. So if you were always told at school that your presentation was rubbish, or that your attitude was wrong, don't be disheartened. Find yourself a career where they place less value on those things, and more value on the things you're good at. There's a career for everyone out there somewhere, whatever your own personal mix of talents and attitudes. Trust yourself, whether you're still learning or whether you've moved on, and play to your strengths.

And if you've spent the whole of this Rule thinking it was written just for you, because you're a non-conformist with rubbish handwriting, take my advice and don't go into teaching.

RULE 9
Getting on at school is not the same as getting on in life

"Have something to say for yourself"

Here's something I get asked about frequently. If you're fundamentally shy and find it hard to make friends, social occasions can be very daunting. Whether it's talking to people generally, or specifically members of the opposite sex, or senior managers at work, it can be a terrifying prospect. What will you say? What if you dry up? Suppose you make a fool of yourself?

I have to declare upfront that this isn't a difficulty I struggle with myself. I'll talk to anyone, me. Some might even say I overdo it. But I have had many friends who face this problem, sometimes daily, and I've seen how crippling it can become.

I have also frequently watched people at social gatherings to see how they deal with making polite conversation. And I can tell you that the people who are most successful at it are the ones who aim not to talk, but to listen. All you need are a few questions to get the other person started, and then let them do the talking. Sooner or later, unless they're very deeply tedious, they'll say something that really catches your imagination, and you can go off script and ask them for more information. Once you're engaged in this way, you'll probably find that you start joining in and, before you know it, you'll be engrossed in a conversation without trying. But even if you're still a bit inhibited, you can carry on doing more than your share of listening.

People love talking about themselves, and their thoughts and experiences and ideas. No one will mind you encouraging them to do most of the talking, and most will really enjoy it and appreciate your interest. And people really are interesting. All of them, in one way or another.

I remember an old family friend a generation or so older than me. I used to dread getting lumbered with him at social events.

He seemed to me to have a drab job and a drab life. Then, one day, he started telling me about his theory of spiders, and how the reason most of us are afraid of them is because we instinctively recognize that they're an alien species. They come from another planet . . . He really had me hooked after that, I can tell you. I didn't know which was more interesting – the theory, or the fact that such an unlikely person should subscribe to it.

The other thing about this approach is that it takes your focus off yourself and puts it firmly on the other person. And when you're not thinking about your shyness, you have a far better chance of relaxing and getting stuck into the conversation.

If you know who you're going to be meeting, prepare a few relevant questions ('I've heard you're a keen tennis player . . .', or whatever). If you don't know who you'll meet, have a standard list of questions you can ask people. Everyone loves to talk about their passions, so try to find out what those are (for example, 'What do you do when you're not at work?'). That way you should barely need to speak at all until you're ready to. And in the meantime – well, everyone likes a good listener.

RULE 10
If you find it hard to talk, try listening

"Some people are just difficult"

Some people seem to be downright unpleasant. Maybe they're always winding other people up, or they won't stop bragging about how smart or clever or sporty or rich they are. Could be that they like stirring up trouble and passing on things told to them in confidence. They end up losing friends over it – or not acquiring friends in the first place.

So why do they do it, if it means very few people like them? No one likes to be unpopular. I'm not talking about the people who have plenty of friends but you're not one of them. I'm talking about the people who know they're unpopular, but still keep boasting or niggling or irritating regardless.

There has to be a reason, you know. People don't act in a way that alienates others without some sort of reason driving them to do it. That's not rational. So when you encounter people like this, try to work out what's behind their behaviour. Why? Are you asking me why you should bother? Well, because you're a Rules player, that's why.

Listen, these people need help. And it costs you nothing to think about how you can help them. Maybe they want attention, maybe they feel insecure – people who keep telling you how great they are, are talking to themselves, even if they don't recognize the fact. They're insecure and they're trying to reassure themselves that they're OK. Lots of people feel small, and try to big themselves up by putting other people down. It's not clever, and it's not the right way to deal with it, but you can kind of see where they're coming from.

If you can start to see what drives these people's behaviour, it's easier for you to cope with it. It may still be a pain, but it should be a bit more bearable. That in itself is a good reason to put yourself in their shoes.

On top of that, maybe you can help to give them what they need. For example, the natural tendency with big-heads is to put them down. Quite understandable. But counter-productive. If you do that, they'll need to big themselves up even more, so they'll get worse and not better. Far better to force yourself to give them credit when they deserve it, much as it may stick in your craw. Comment on how well-organized their launch event was, or how well written you found their report, or how well they fielded at Saturday's match, or how you envy their talent at interior décor. Yes, I know you don't want to, but you'll be doing everyone a favour.

It won't always work, but you should feel better for having tried. People with these kinds of tendencies often have parents who rarely show approval, or partners who are pushing them harder than they can cope with, or some other circumstance which may not justify their behaviour, but could in part explain it. Often it's too big an issue for you alone to put right for them, but a bit of kindness from a Rules player who's big enough to do it can count for a lot. Go on, give it a go. What have you got to lose?

RULE 11

No one chooses to be difficult without a reason

"Don't waste your time on people who aren't worth it"

I worked with a young man years ago who was notoriously sullen and taciturn. I was new to the job, and everyone told me there was just no point trying to hold a conversation with him – I'd be wasting my time. They seemed to be right. It was well-nigh impossible to get so much as a grunt out of him.

For some reason I took this as a personal challenge. I don't really know why – certainly not out of any virtuous motive. Anyway, I used to ask him questions and not give up until I had an answer. Then I started asking more open questions, which required fuller answers. After a couple of months, he'd relented to the point where I could hold a good conversation with him.

And you know what? He turned out to be a great guy. Other people started chatting to him and he opened up, and after about six months he was very popular. It turned out he wasn't sullen at all, just painfully inhibited, and unbeknown to us all he'd been going through a terrible time at home. Once he'd gained his confidence, he really benefited from the support of all his 'new' friends, and we all benefited from having him as a mate.

Despite having done this for all the wrong reasons, I learnt a valuable lesson. Time invested in people is never wasted. Sometimes you don't see the results yourself, sometimes you do, but either way the other person will gain from your attention and friendship. You can think you're wasting your time on someone and discover years later how much difference you made to that person's self-esteem or confidence.

Some people are taciturn, like my friend, and others can seem like too much effort because they're belligerent or stupid or immature or irritating. But who knows what lurks beneath all that stuff unless you take the trouble to find out? You don't have to become best friends, but you can certainly give them the time of day and treat them well. Most negative qualities are there for a reason, and there may be secrets in someone's past that explain why they come across as they do.

Look, let's be honest. Sometimes you won't get anywhere with a particular person. You may find out that you've gone out of your way for someone only to find you get snubbed or are unappreciated. Or worse (rarely, I'm relieved to say) that a person has been very rude to you or slighted you behind your back. So *that* person wasn't worth it, were they? Nope, doesn't change a thing. You did the right thing, and kept the moral high ground, and that's what matters.

It really isn't for us to judge who is and isn't worth our time. As Rules players we treat everyone well, and don't question whether they 'deserve' it. It doesn't hurt us and, once in a while, you may discover a good and loyal friend where you never expected to. And that's a great feeling.

RULE 12

Suffer fools gladly. Well, suffer them, anyway

"You can't be cheerful if you're in pain"

Pain grinds you down, makes you grumpy, frustrates you, limits you, and makes you feel hard done by. It's impossible to enjoy life.

Or is it? There obviously must be a level of pain where that's so, but for most people it's perfectly possible to be cheerful regardless. Whether you have a headache, a stinking cold, arthritis, toothache, a broken wrist or a slipped disc, you don't have to be miserable as well.

I had a very enlightening conversation with a friend who has chronic arthritis. I asked her one day, 'Does it hurt all the time?' And she replied, 'Oh, it doesn't hurt! It just aches, that's all'. Now, most people would consider constant aching to be pain. But she has chosen to redefine it so that she doesn't think of herself as being in pain. Much impressed, I've adopted this approach every time I've been in pain since. And she's quite right. If you tell yourself it hurts, it's far more painful than if you tell yourself it doesn't.

You must have noticed that if you're feeling fed up and tired, crammed on a commuter train at the end of a long day, and someone treads heavily on your foot, you can find it really painful. But if you're busy playing football, or enjoying a romantic walk in the countryside, or in the middle of an uplifting open-air concert, you'd barely notice the self-same injury. Which just goes to show that pain is largely in the mind. If you allow it to take over and dictate your mood, it will drag you down. So don't let it.

It just isn't fair on you, or on everyone around you, to be grumpy and downbeat just because some bit of you hurts. When you're young it may seem like bad luck but, trust me, once you get older it's pretty much the norm to have some part of your body letting you down and failing to co-operate. If that's all it takes to spoil your fun, life's going to go downhill fast once you pass about 40 or 50.

The time to practise getting the better of pain is, ideally, when you're young. For most younger people, most of the time, it's an irregular occurrence. Nothing to moan about compared with some of the people you know. So get into the habit of telling yourself that your headache isn't that bad, or your tooth only aches a bit, or your bad knee isn't enough to stop you walking, or the eczema is itchy but it doesn't really hurt. Accept that it is what it is, and then just get on with your life.

If you focus deeply on the pain, you can try to analyze it to the point where you can 'zen' it, and it becomes impossible to explain to yourself why it 'hurts'. It's just a sensation you're experiencing. Very interesting. And now let's get back to what you were doing and pay it no further mind.

RULE 13

Pain doesn't have to make you miserable

"Good work speaks for itself"

When I was growing up, it was considered very bad manners to show anything other than modesty, all the time, even if it was false modesty. The idea was that people could see for themselves what your skills, talents, gifts, strengths, achievements and successes were, without you having to point them out to them.

Now on a social level, this is broadly a good principle, although I don't hold with false modesty, and it's perfectly possible to be politely humble without being meek. The alternative is being a braggart, and that's never welcomed by the people around you.

However, when it comes to work, you just can't assume that your bosses will notice what you've been up to, or realize that it was you who suggested that particularly effective new system, or remember the great piece of work you produced last February. You have to tell them.

I've known people languish on slow career ladders for years, wondering why other people are being promoted ahead of them, when the reason is quite simply that they're not bringing their successes to the attention of the boss – or the boss's boss. Look, in this modern world, management people don't have time to sit around reflecting on what their team members have been up to. They haven't got time to look at anything if it's not under their noses. So if you want them to see what you're up to, put it right there under their nose. And then point at it.

Of course you're still not allowed to brag. That doesn't go down well with anyone. You can't walk the office corridor singing, 'I'm the best salesperson they've ever had!' at the top of your voice and expect to be liked. And being liked matters – management won't want to promote you if you're universally unpopular. So how are you going to ensure that the bosses know all the good stuff you've been up to?

For a start you can make sure you attach your name clearly (but not ostentatiously) to every piece of written work you do. Send round emails after particular successes. No, not emails that say, 'Wasn't I brilliant?' but ones that are relevant – asking for feedback, drawing attention to a significant sale or coup, passing on feedback from customers. You can even copy the boss in to your email thanking your team. They all make the point that you were responsible, without bragging. Make sure you mention the things you're proudest of at your appraisal, in case your boss has forgotten them. And if you're achieving particular success with a new system, approach, strategy or technique of your own devising, write an unsolicited report about how the company could benefit if they introduced it across the board.

You see? None of these things will make your grandmother cringe at your pushiness or boastfulness, but they will ensure that your strengths get noticed so that next time there's a promotion or a pay rise in the offing . . . well, your name will be remembered.

And there's just one more thing you need to do to make all this effort worthwhile. Be damn good at your job.

RULE 14

No one at work will know how good you are unless you tell them

---

"Do what it takes to get what you want"

How do you feel when people use emotional blackmail against you? They try to get you to lie for them because they'll be in such trouble if you don't, or they ask you to lend them money because they really need to buy their poor gran a birthday present, or they put you under pressure to come to a party you clearly don't want to attend because they'll feel really uncomfortable if they don't know anyone there.

If you're anything like me, you feel resentful when this happens, slightly annoyed at being taken advantage of, and less willing to do whatever the person is asking. And yet often we still concede because the person makes it so difficult for us to say no without appearing rude or unsupportive. Some people say yes out of guilt.* That's the intention of course – the emotional blackmailer doesn't care how we feel, so long as they get what they want.

What always surprises me slightly is that although we all hate being emotionally blackmailed, some people seem to have no compunction about doing it to others. My observation is that, because it's ostensibly a fairly subtle manipulation, they think that they won't be spotted, that the person they're talking to won't recognize it as emotional blackmail this time, so it will be OK.

Well, that's just plain wrong. We all know when we're being blackmailed, because we're being put under pressure to do something we don't want to do. When we say no, we mean no. If someone doesn't accept that answer, and piles on the pressure, we always feel uncomfortable and resistant no matter what method

---

* Rule 85 will go into that thorny topic. No, no, don't skip. Wait until you get there.

they employ. So our antennae are switched on and we can spot emotional blackmail a mile off.

Now listen. Emotional blackmail is a form of coercion, and as Rules players we just don't do it. We don't use any form of coercion: physical, emotional, financial, psychological or anything else. If someone says no, we accept it.

Yes, I know you'll be in huge trouble if your friend won't cover up for you, I know your gran would really like a birthday present and you're skint, I know you'll hate the party if you don't know anyone. I'm not suggesting that you're lying. I simply don't care that you're telling the truth. That doesn't make it OK. You're focusing on how you feel and what you want, and ignoring the feelings of the person you're pressurizing. And that's not nice, is it? Make your request, state the facts, keep it unemotional, and be prepared to take no for an answer.

RULE 15

Don't emotionally blackmail people

"A place for everything, and everything in its place"

I was brought up to consider that I 'ought' to get up early, keep my house tidy, say no to chocolate, and plenty of other such beliefs. The adults around me were attaching a moral value to issues which just don't have a moral dimension.

It's tough enough working hard, being nice and trying to leave the world a better place. It's quite unnecessary to load ourselves with all sorts of other spurious standards that just make day-to-day living harder – without benefiting anyone. Why should I have to be tidy if I don't want to, in my own house? Of course I don't drop litter in the street, but I should be free to leave my washing-up until morning. There's no moral issue there. It's not good or bad or virtuous or sinful. It just takes a bit more elbow grease to get it clean if I haven't soaked it, but that's my choice.

Don't let anyone brainwash you into feeling you're at fault in some way if you want to have a lie-in, for example. So long as you don't have to be anywhere else, you can get up as late as you like. It isn't 'good' to get up early. I used to live in a small village where the little old dear next door to me would often say, 'I notice your curtains weren't opened until 10 o'clock this morning', in a disapproving tone, as though I was a naughty child.

I had a relative who, whenever you offered her a chocolate, would always say, 'Ooh, I shouldn't . . .' and then reach into the box, saying 'It is naughty of me'. No! It's not! It's just a chocolate – eat it if you want to, and not if you don't. But don't get all moral about it.

One of the most frustrating things about some of these false morals is that they become so universally accepted that they can seriously hamper relationships. Very few couples have the same standards of tidiness, for example. That should be fine, and a matter for negotiation over what degree of mess the couple will tolerate in the house, and who will do something about it if it starts to exceed this level. That's quite enough to have to agree on. In fact, however, what almost always happens is that the whole discussion is conducted under the assumption that the tidier person is somehow morally in the right, and the messier partner is inherently wrong. Why? Think it through, and then try to work out why it's any 'better' to be tidy. It may be more practical, or help you find things quicker, or stop you tripping over the furniture. But on the other hand, it's more effort, it's less relaxed and it wastes time. Morals don't come into it. It's simply a matter of preference.

Once you start looking out for these things, you may find yourself carrying around all sorts of moral baggage that you don't need. Everyone's parents and teachers impose such values, on top of the genuinely moral ones that they hopefully imbue you with. So question, all the time, and don't let anyone guilt-trip you about things that affect no one but yourself.

RULE 16

It's not morally superior to be tidy

"It matters what other people think"

No, no, no. It matters what *you* think. What you think deep down, I mean – not what you'd like to think. The only sure way to navigate through life is to have your own compass. Then if you want to know whether you're on track, you have only to refer to yourself.

I have a close friend who is constantly dissatisfied with herself. No matter how well she does at work, she always feels she should have done better. She's a great mum, but constantly thinks she's messing up at home too. Why? Because her own mother either tells her she's not doing enough, or implies it by withholding praise and approval when my friend does well.

One of my half-brothers, who lost his father when he was very young, has spent his whole life looking for his dad's approval. Sadly he'll never get it. Which means that until he learns to find approval within himself he'll be forever frustrated, striving for something that doesn't exist. No amount of achievement – personal, social, work or anything else – will make him feel satisfied.

Far too many of us fall into this kind of trap. Confidence is a big part of it, and that's hard to find when you're being undermined by the people you've come to accept as arbiters of your achievements. But you need to find that confidence, and learn to trust your own judgement. If necessary, spend less time around the people who judge you harshly, and cultivate friends, family and mentors who encourage you. That's to build you up, not to replace one set of judges with another, better set, because in the end you're the only judge who matters. I know this can be really tough, but the rewards are worthwhile.

The fact is that you need your own clear values and principles regardless of what other people say. Even if you're surrounded by positive support, you still need to be able to judge your own actions for yourself. Only then can you feel comfortable with yourself in the darkest of times, or facing the hardest of decisions. So to get through life successfully, you'll have to find the confidence to trust yourself regardless of what other people think.

I'm not saying you shouldn't feel a glow when someone you respect shows their approval. Please enjoy it. But also learn to enjoy the achievement without the need for other people's endorsement.

RULE 17
Don't live for other people's approval

"Give as good as you get"

Have you ever been metaphorically slapped in the face by someone you've treated with care and kindness? Most of us have, and it's easy to wish that you hadn't bothered with them. I used to have two neighbours, both elderly women (sadly long gone now). They were good friends, and one day Elsie had arranged to have Phyllis over for lunch. About half an hour before she was due to arrive, Phyllis phoned her and said, 'I'm not coming to lunch, and you needn't bother asking me again'. Then she hung up. Now, this was 15 years before I moved into the neighbourhood, but when I met Elsie all those years later, she still had no idea what she'd done. Phyllis hadn't spoken to her since.

Poor Elsie felt dreadful about this, and you could understand her thinking twice about friendships in the future. But she was naturally a very giving person, and she didn't allow the experience to change her. She continued to show kindness and generosity to people around her, and we loved having her as a neighbour. She was popular and her house was always full of people. As she got older and more frail, she always had plenty of friends to support her.

This is a bit like some folk tale, apart from it being true. The plot is just as predictable: Phyllis was indeed fairly sour and difficult, and over the years she alienated almost all her neighbours, and was left with few friends. She's the only neighbour I've ever fallen out with, and I'm not entirely sure how I incurred her displeasure.

Now we've all heard stories of this kind before but, like this one, they really do happen in real life. Again and again and again. If you're kind, helpful and thoughtful, you'll have loads of friends and lots of support when you need it. As with Elsie, the positive stuff doesn't always come back from the people you gave it to, but it comes back from somewhere.

Think of it like karma. My son has a friend whose dad gives him a lift to school very early once a week, because we can't get him there otherwise. I sometimes feel bad that I can't return the favour, although the dad in question really doesn't care – he's a generous guy and simply happy to help. However, I let another friend's child stay over with us occasionally on a school night to help out, and there isn't a favour I need from them in return. I figure we're all helping each other in some sort of chain, and as long as we're all happy to help someone – not necessarily the person who's helping us – we're all earning positive karma and the system works.

You have no way of knowing who you'll want help or support from in the future, so just keep building up that karma, and it will come back to you when you need it most.

RULE 18
You get what you give

"Stick with your own kind"

When I was in my early twenties, I worked for a while in an industry where people came from all sorts of backgrounds. Seventy-year-olds from the rough end of town rubbed shoulders with 20-year-old toffs. Thirty-year-olds were often in charge of 50-year-olds. People with top degrees hung out with others who had left school at 16 without two decent exam results to rub together.

It was wonderfully liberating, hugely educational and enormous fun. It's easy to spend most of your life with people about your age, who do the same kind of thing you do, and have similar interests away from work. But while friendships with these people may be easy, they're also, well . . . easy. It's far more interesting to spend some of your time with people who are very different from you.

I'm not suggesting you dump all your old school friends. Far from it. Some of them may be wonderful and they should be cultivated. But do your best to put yourself in situations where you can make new friends who are a bit more challenging. I don't mean they'll be tricky people (some might), but having a very different background – whether in terms of generation, education, class or anything else – means they'll have a set of attitudes and values that may be unlike your own. And that's a good thing, because it will make you think.

We're all blinkered to some extent. It's unavoidable. No one can know what the world is like all over. Mother Teresa probably had very little experience of what it was like living on a ranch in the Australian outback. But the more forays you make into lives that are different from your own, the more you understand other people – and the more that sheds light on your own life. Not to mention that you also discover that people are fundamentally the same everywhere, and you'll find just as good friends in unusual places, if you look for them.

Some people are harder work to stay friends with – and a few may not be worth it. But it's important you don't dismiss people who aren't like you, because you'll miss out on some of the most rewarding friendships that way. Maybe they come from a world unlike your own, or maybe they have different interests or attitudes from yours. If you really have nothing to share with each other, you can just wave and smile. But see if there isn't more common ground than you recognize at first. Often the unlikeliest friends can be the best.

RULE 19
Your friends don't all need to be like you

"The best things in life are free"

OK, so a few good things in life come to you for nothing. But you have no control over what they are, or when they arrive. Sometimes you don't even recognize them when they happen. The things that are *really* worth having – they take effort.

The things that are most worthwhile are friends and family. People don't come free. At the risk of sounding both sugary and depressing at the same time,* love hurts. That's kind of the point. It's what makes it so good when it's going well. There's no such thing as a relationship that's easy. People say that you have to work at relationships, which doesn't make much sense until you've done it. But it's true – you have to compromise and sacrifice to keep a relationship strong. If it's a good relationship, your partner will be doing exactly the same thing. And the whole thing with sacrifices is that they hurt – otherwise they wouldn't be sacrifices (duh). But they'll be worth it too, or you wouldn't bother.

It's the same with children (if you don't have them or even want them, read this from your parents' perspective – actually, do that anyway). Every time things go wrong for them, it breaks your heart. Every time you think about how fragile their lives are, you just want to hold onto them and never let go. But you have to let them go, let them make their own mistakes, let them take risks, and all you can do is stand back and watch and hold your breath. Of course it hurts. Every day. But that's because you love them so much – and that's what makes all the hurt worthwhile.

You can't run away from it. The only way to avoid it is to avoid life. Don't get involved, don't talk to anyone, don't go anywhere, don't look at anything. And what's the point of that? No, you

---

* See – I can multitask, even though I'm a bloke.

simply have to jump in with both feet, and grit your teeth against the pain. And it is worth it, it really is. And the thing that makes it so wonderfully, excitingly, vibrantly worthwhile is all the pain you had to go through to get there.

I'm not saying that it hurts all the time. Some things would hurt if you thought about them, but you don't have to keep thinking about them. There will be lots of good times when everything is going swimmingly. But sooner or later, those things you really care about will bring you pain.

It's yin and yang. You can't have one without having a bit of the other. The darkest times have some light in them, and the best times in your life will have a little spot of pain in them. And that's as it should be.

RULE 20
Everything worth having hurts

"You can change people"

It's astounding how many people believe this – maybe because they really want to. It's very tempting to find someone who is 95 per cent of the way to being the partner you want, and then trying to tweak the last 5 per cent into place. If only they were just a bit tougher, or a little bit less flighty, or more tolerant, or less of a spendthrift, or a bit more of a risk-taker. Wouldn't that be perfect?

Now look at it the other way around. Suppose you meet someone who thinks you're almost perfect, but who sets out to turn you into their perfect man or woman. They'd prefer you a bit tougher, or a little bit less flighty, or more tolerant . . . How do you feel about that? And do you think it would be possible to change who you are?

However you look at it, trying to change someone is another way of saying there's something wrong with them. Partner or friend, it undermines their confidence and makes them feel criticized and got at. And it's very controlling too.

All of which might explain why trying to change other people always backfires. And what's more, it doesn't work. Most of us simply can't change our basic nature, however much we try. We can change our outward behaviour of course – and it's usually reasonable to ask someone close to adjust their behaviour if you have a good reason and ask nicely – but underlying character is a very different business.

Listen, I'm not moralizing here. I'm not saying you should or you shouldn't. I'm just saying that – right or wrong – it won't give you what you want. I've seen people try it, and I've seen people lose their confidence and their self-esteem trying to be something they're not. But I've never seen a successful relationship or friendship founded on changing each other. Every really successful one

I've seen has been based on two people accepting each other for what they are, and learning to live with the 5 per cent because the 95 per cent is more than worth it.

If you've found someone who is 95 per cent of the partner you want, you're doing well. So long as the other 5 per cent isn't a predilection for pulling the wings off baby birds, but is simply a reasonable trait that doesn't happen to be on your own personal checklist, 95 per cent is a very high mark already. If someone needs to change, then it will have to be you. You'll need to change your response to that 5 per cent so that it doesn't spoil everything. If you can do that, you'll have a great relationship. If you can't, well, that should demonstrate how unrealistic it is to expect them to change.

Don't forget, you're probably 5 per cent short of their ideal partner too, and they'll also have to change their response to that if this is going to work. Isn't that enough, without asking them to change their personality too?

RULE 21
Don't try to change people

"It's where you're going that matters, not where you came from"

I grew up on the edge of Brixton, a notoriously insalubrious part of London. Whenever I was asked where I lived my mother would hiss at me, 'Say *Dulwich*' (Brixton's better appointed neighbour). This isn't an unusual attitude – many people are ashamed to admit where they come from. Plenty of people work to disguise a regional accent, or change their dialect, all to ensure that no one realizes where they grew up.

Of course you can go too far the other way. I had a good friend when I was younger who came from a rough part of Manchester. She was the first in her family to stay at school until she was 18, and then got a good job in the city centre with a decent salary. Some members of her family made it clear they saw her as a traitor to her working class roots, hanging out with all her new friends. She really wasn't ashamed of her background, and made no attempt to hide it. She just wanted to get on in life.

Where you come from is a part of you. You can choose to stay there all your life, or you can choose to move around and end up somewhere very different. Both of those options are fine. But if you try to hide your roots, you're denying a part of yourself. And sooner or later that will make you unhappy. You'll regret being ashamed, or you'll live in fear of being found out.

If your background is humble, that speaks all the more loudly of your achievements when you succeed (in your own terms of course) against such odds. Why would you want to hide that? We all know prejudice exists, but anyone who is so shallow they'll judge you on something you have no control over – where you were born – isn't worth your time or respect (although being a

Rules player you'll remain civil at all times). It's as wrongheaded and prejudiced as judging you on the colour of your skin.

There are places where it's seen as more embarrassing to admit that you're privileged than to acknowledge a poor background. But it's still a part of you, and it's daft to be ashamed of the fortune you were born into. That suggests that you disdain other people who aspire to your advantages, which is patronizing and *would* be something to keep quiet about. No, if you're ashamed, you need to consider why. If you feel such advantage is unfair (I can't comment – I have no idea how privileged you really are) then do something to redress the balance. Get some experience of how the other half lives, do what you can to spread your kind of advantages (wealth, education, a supportive family) more fairly around the world, whether in your own small area or in some wider way – work, charity, informally, whatever feels right for you. And don't allow inverted snobs to make you feel ashamed of your lucky beginnings.

So be happy to stand up and declare your roots. Remember what they've taught you, the opportunities they've given you, the strength you've developed to make the best of them, and be proud of them, because they're a part of you.

RULE 22
Be proud of your roots

"Friends are for life"

Apparently we can all manage to maintain a relationship with around 150 friends. It's called Dunbar's Number, after the scientist who identified it. Actually, it's not an exact number, and could lie anywhere between 100 and 230, but that doesn't matter. The point is that it's finite. We're talking here about proper friends, people you can have a meaningful relationship with, who you can interact with. We're not talking about the number of people who might be following you on Twitter or Facebook, or who you'd nod at if you passed them in the street.

As you go through life, you meet new people. Some of them you like more than others. A few of them become friends. After the next job or holiday or social event you might add someone else, and someone else. Pretty soon, you're going to find you've already got 150 friends. So what happens when you add more?

I'll tell you what happens. People drop off the bottom of the list. It's not a conscious thing. You don't come home from a party thinking, 'I really liked that chap I met. We swapped numbers and I'd like to keep in touch. Hmmm – who shall I drop from my friends list to make room?' No, you don't even notice it happening. But every so often you find yourself thinking that you haven't seen someone for a while, or that you really must make the effort to call so-and-so.

This is natural, and the way things are. You don't have to feel guilty about it. Yes, if you haven't phoned your best mate who's going through a dreadful time you probably should hurry up and call them. But if you haven't been in touch with some friend you used to work with who moved away, well, they haven't been in touch with you either, and maybe your time together has been and gone. And that's OK.

People move in and out of each other's lives, and that's the way it is. The more everyone moves around, the more fluid friendship groups can become. In traditional communities, 150 people might be your village, and you might never move away. But in the modern world this is less and less the case, and you will lose touch with some friends. You'll make sure you keep in contact with the ones who matter most to you, and sometimes people magically and wonderfully come back into your life after years apart. Sometimes you lose all trace of someone, or you keep track of them through someone else but the real friendship fades.

This sounds sad, but the reason for it is that new people are becoming important to you, and giving you the support, fun and company that you need. And the same thing is happening for the people dropping quietly off the bottom of your list. So it's OK. In fact it's a good thing. There are always new friends waiting up ahead. So work to keep the friends that you really want to hang on to, but don't feel bad when others drift away.

RULE 23

Friends come and go

"Mistakes are a bad thing"

Back in the 1920s, lots of medical people were studying influenza. My great-grandfather was one of them. He, like many others, was frustrated that the culture dishes he was using kept getting contaminated with a mould that destroyed the bacteria around it. Annoyed that he couldn't get the cultures to develop properly, he threw the dishes away and started again. This happened frequently, and like many other doctors he kept having to throw away these faulty cultures. One scientist, however, Alexander Fleming, realized that a mould that destroyed bacteria wasn't actually a frustrating mistake, but a valuable discovery. He abandoned his original study, and started developing the mould instead. He called it penicillin.

And that explains why you'll find Fleming in history books the world over, but my great-grandfather doesn't get a mention. Fleming's attitude to mistakes was that you could learn something from them, while my great-grandfather was too busy berating himself for messing up to see what was under his nose.

There are plenty more modest examples of this same principle. Right at the other end of the scale, I never truly appreciated the rationale behind filling up the car with petrol regularly until the time I ran out at 3am on a cold, wet night. That may sound like a flippant example, but it shows that we make mistakes at every level, and that's how we learn. If you watch a toddler trying to stick two Lego bricks together, you'll see that they can't do it properly until they've got it wrong a few times.

Want more examples? My second marriage is strong partly because I learnt from the mistakes I made first time around. I have a friend who messed up all through school and came out with no qualifications. It was his inability to get the kind of jobs he wanted, and knew he could do, that drove him to go back to college and work doubly hard to get great results. He'd never have done so well if he'd worked at school and then gone onto college without such drive and motivation. Some people might, but for him the mistakes he made early on became his motivation. Sometimes mistakes are the only way we can learn – and so long as we recognize where we've gone wrong, mistakes can lead us to great places we'd never have found otherwise.

The important thing about mistakes isn't to avoid them but to make sure you learn from them. Avoiding them studiously is a bad idea, because you rarely succeed if you never take any risks. As Einstein said, 'A person who never made a mistake never tried anything new'. The more mistakes you make – so long as you're learning from them – the more interesting a life you're living. And that's got to be good.

RULE 24
Mistakes can be good

"Be a friend to everybody"

We're good, decent people, you and me. We're Rules players, aren't we? So surely we should treat everybody well – like everyone we meet. Actually, yes . . . and no. Treat everybody well, certainly, but we don't have to like everyone.

If we're playing by the Rules, we probably will like most people. We'll be open and amicable, we'll do our best to be understanding, we'll be helpful and charming and kind and co-operative and considerate. That brings out the best in people, so we'll see the most likeable side of almost everyone we encounter.

But there are always exceptions. I know someone who claims to dislike only three people. As far as I can tell, that's genuinely true. She's a Rules player, and I should think that's more people than dislike her. However, some people have traits that really rub you up the wrong way, or you meet them under unfortunate circumstances. You're dating their ex, or you have started a new job only to find someone working under you who applied for it unsuccessfully and resents you. I imagine they won't show you their best side. And sometimes they'll behave in ways that make it impossible for you to like them.

Personally I find there are very few people I actively dislike, but there have been a handful in my life. Not to mention several I wouldn't go so far as to say I dislike, but I don't actively like them. Whether or not you like someone is a feeling, and you can't help how you feel. So as long as you've given someone your best shot, don't feel obliged to like them.

Ah, but how you treat them – that's a different matter. As a Rules player, you should make it your mission to conceal your dislike. Always be civil, mannerly and considerate regardless of your personal feelings. After all, you'll only make things worse if you don't, and a Rules player occupies the moral high ground at all times. Make sure they have nothing to reproach you with.

There will just once in a while be times when you feel you have to express a strong opposing view out of principle. Maybe you're standing up to someone who is victimizing another person. On these – hopefully rare – occasions you are free to say exactly how you feel about their behaviour, but don't tell them you dislike them. How will that help? Not only is it unnecessary, but it makes your attack seem personal, which undermines its authority. Keep it objective.

These occasions should be few and far between, however. The rest of the time just act as if you like everyone. Apart from being the most civilized way to behave, you'll also find people much more likeable, and you'll enjoy them more.

RULE 25
You don't have to like everyone

" . . . and everybody will be your friend"

As we saw in the last Rule, there will be people who don't like you. Who knows why . . .? Maybe you have some habit that doesn't irritate most people, but really gets to them. Perhaps they're jealous. Or they have some misconception about you. Or your relationship to them isn't conducive to liking each other – maybe you have some position of authority over them that they resent, or perhaps they dislike your brother or uncle or friends and are tarring you with the same brush.

Needing to be liked is a common characteristic, and it can help us to make friends. Clearly you're more likely to be popular if you want to be than if you don't give two hoots. However, many people who want to be liked find it hard to cope with being disliked, even by people who they dislike themselves. Now, that's just not logical. OK, I agree that feelings aren't logical and shouldn't have to be, but I want to spell out what an unrealistic position this is. Once you recognize how daft it is, you may find it easier to overcome.

Think about it. If you don't like someone, why would you care what they think of you? Why is their opinion of any interest? In some cases, it's even flattering to be disliked by someone you have no respect for. The fact is that if you're happy and comfortable in the relationships and friendships you have, if you're satisfied that you're playing by the Rules, if you have no regrets or embarrassment or shame about the way you behave, you won't allow other people's judgement of you to colour your self-judgement. In other words, if you're confident in yourself, you'll be able to shrug off other people's dislike and tell yourself, 'That's just the way they are. It's nothing to do with me'.

Sometimes you want to be liked by someone because you have a great deal of respect for them. As a Rules player you will not often find yourself disliked, especially by those you admire. What is more likely to apply, if you're under-confident, is that you'll think people dislike you when in fact they don't. So confidence is the key to overcoming this too.

Over time, following the Rules will give you confidence. It won't come overnight, but when you realize you're living your life well, and doing your best by other people, you'll come to feel more comfortable in your own skin. Hang out with the right people – people you respect and who build you up – tackle any demons in your past that hamper your self-image, and you will eventually get to a point where it doesn't matter to you if a few people, who you have little to do with, don't particularly like you. So what?

RULE 26

. . . and not everyone will like you

"If you don't like it, tough"

How many times do you hear people say that they're unhappy with their job/university course/relationship/house/car or whatever, but they're stuck with it? You may well have said it yourself. The problem with this attitude is that it makes you a victim. You have no control over your circumstances and you simply have to put up with whatever fate has thrown at you.

Look, if you take this attitude, it's hardly surprising if you feel miserable, anxious and trapped. Who wouldn't? If there's really nothing you can do to extricate yourself from this thing that's making you so unhappy, that's immensely frustrating. But highly unlikely.

Are you so sure there isn't an alternative? That's very rarely the case, unless you're in prison, for example, or caught in the kind of poverty trap that is relatively unusual, at least in the West, and in which case you're not likely to be reading this book. Actually, there's almost always an alternative.

You could switch courses. You could jack in the job. You could move house, work on the relationship – or end it – and get rid of the car. If you're feeling trapped, I recommend you think carefully about your options.

I have a friend whose daughter went to a new school at 16. After a few months, she was really unhappy, and felt trapped on a course she wasn't enjoying, because she wanted the qualifications at the end of it. The teaching was fine at her school, but she didn't fit in well socially and wasn't making any close friends. So she decided to go and look around the college in a nearby town. She found out about transport to get there, and asked about available courses, and how she would swap over.

She discovered that it was possible to change courses. The travel would take longer, but otherwise it would work fine. But the more she thought about it, the more she realized that actually she was OK where she was. The teaching was good, the school was close, which was important, and all in all she just didn't want to risk changing. She decided to stay where she was. She concentrated on existing friendships outside school, and treated her course as a place to work rather than socialize.

So she ended up doing exactly the same as before, but now she was happy doing it. Why? Because she was *choosing* to stay there, rather than feeling trapped. She was taking control of her life, and it was an active decision to stay put.

That's why you should consider all your options. You may end up back where you started, but if you stop playing the victim and put yourself in control instead, by actively looking at the alternatives, you should find you're much more ready to appreciate what you have. Or, of course, you might end up making changes to your life. And that's fine too. Just don't moan that you have no choice, that you're stuck – because that's almost never the case.

RULE 27

Remember, you have a choice

"You need to get your chores over with"

Sometimes it seems as if life is full of minor irritations and frustrations, none of which is actually in the least important. Putting the laundry through, getting that report finished, checking the oil in the car, buying more bread because it's running out before the weekly shop, phoning your mum, rearranging an appointment, paying a bill, finishing an essay, posting a letter. Lots of them involve other people too – you have to keep calling someone until you catch them, you can't rearrange the appointment until you've spoken to your boss, you need to speak to your tutor before you can complete the essay.

Wouldn't it be great if all these little things would stop getting in the way, and you could actually find the time to live life properly? If you added up all the time you spend on these inconsequential actions and interactions, you'd have so much more time to enjoy life.

You might think that, but you'd be wrong. Because, strange as it may seem, all those million tiny actions and preoccupations are in fact what constitute life. Like a pointillist painting, all those little dots – if viewed from a great enough distance – make up the big picture. And that's a good thing. Take them away, and actually there's nothing much left. A close friend of mine who lost her husband tells me that for a while after he died, she really resented the everyday niggles and necessities of life. She just ignored them for a few weeks because she could – for once no one expected anything of her. But once they'd faded into the background, she found there was nothing to replace them. She realized that they weren't, in fact, a negative frustration. They were a positive thing that needed to be embraced. The spaces between things turned out to be more important than the things themselves.

That's not to say that there aren't any big things, but most of them are made up of little things. You might devote your whole life to charity, but you'd still be frustrated when the relief parcels didn't arrive on time, or you'd have to nip out to get milk before your next meeting, or remember to feed the cat. Suppose you had a more hedonistic view, and decided life would be one long holiday. There'd still be timetables and tide-tables and food to sort out and running out of clothes and losing your keys.

I'll bet even the Pope has days when he can't work out where his favourite socks have got to. Or the President of the USA has to find time to brief his assistant to dig out all his receipts to give to his accountant. Or the Queen suddenly remembers she meant to give a particular birthday present to a lady-in-waiting and has to sort it out in a hurry. That's life. And I do mean it – that really *is* life. It's all there is in the end. Enjoy it.

RULE 28
Life's all about the little things

"Stay true to your dreams"

When I was younger I wanted to live on a boat. I loved boats. I worked on Scottish fishing trawlers one summer, and my dream was to have my own boat. I'd be wild and free and piratical and adventurous.

Over the years, I've owned many boats. None of them big enough to live on, but enough to enjoy a trip out on when I've had time. Rowing boats and rubber dinghies and fibreglass launches with outboards and canoes and little motorboats. One day, I promised myself, I'd buy a boat big enough to live on. It's nearly happened many times, but somehow it's never quite come to pass.

The thing is, I got married and had kids. I got jobs which didn't leave much time for all the work that living on a boat entails. Or I worked from home and needed electricity and warmth and a postal address. After many, many years, I eventually accepted that, actually, I probably didn't really want to live on a boat any more. I'm still in love with the idea of it, but the reality isn't going to happen, at least not for a very long time.

To begin with, that seemed very sad. That's because I was still coming to terms with it. I now realize that I don't want to live on a boat. If I did, I'd be doing it. I'm very happy just dreaming about living on a boat. One of my grown-up sons lives on a boat, and I can see how much work and hardship it entails. He loves it, but deep down I have this sneaky feeling that I might not enjoy it as much as I think. I can't imagine being trapped on a small floating island with three teenagers, and I've stopped pretending to like being cold and wet these days, and I want to be able to nip out for a paper without waiting for the tide to turn, and not have to get in a boat in the dark and rain in order to get ashore.

I used to feel I'd somehow betrayed my dreams by resigning myself to being a landlubber. I felt I 'should' do the boat thing because that's what I'd said I was going to do all those years ago. But our priorities change, and we need to give ourselves permission to adapt to them, without feeling bad about it.

You may be determined to get to the top in your career, and then wake up one day to find that actually your family is more important. Or resolve to devote your efforts to a particular charity, and then find years later that actually you feel you need to step back so you can put more time into something else. This is fine. No one can know when they're 20 what they'll be doing when they're 60 – or even know when they're 50 what they'll be doing at 60. We change, the world changes, the people around us change. So pursue your goals whatever your stage in life, but be prepared for those goals to shift.

RULE 29
Priorities change over the years

"People have a right to know"

There's nothing more fun than passing on a juicy bit of news to a friend. And sometimes it can help everyone. You can bring people together who hadn't realized they had something in common, or do someone a favour by explaining their situation to the right person. Of course not all gossip is helpful, but it doesn't have to be malicious either. A Rules player never indulges in malicious gossip. And anyway, there's so much benign gossip, why would you need to?

There are more categories than just benign or malicious though, aren't there? There's news that you've been asked not to mention, but in this situation you can't see how it can hurt. There's news that you weren't specifically asked not to discuss, but maybe you weren't intended to pass it on. There's news you've heard indirectly, or news you've stumbled across accidentally.

Some people have big secrets. And some people have secrets that don't seem big at all. In fact you're not at all sure why they're supposed to be secrets. Sometimes you're not sure they *are* as secret as the person thinks. In fact, sometimes, who's to say what really is a secret?

I'll tell you who. The person it's about – the one it originates with. They get to choose how big a secret it is, and it's no one else's business why it matters to them. There's only one Rule you need to follow: keep your mouth shut. If you're in the slightest doubt about how the subject of a piece of information feels about it being shared, just stay quiet.

What if they didn't tell you it themselves? Just stay quiet. Suppose they didn't actually say it was a secret? Keep schtum. What if it's an open secret? Stay mum. What if you don't even like them? That's got nothing to do with it – just keep it to yourself. Suppose it's not important? It might be important to them, so button it. What if . . . Shushhh! There are no ifs, buts, supposes, what ifs. A secret is a secret and if it's not your secret, it's not yours to divulge.

Some people care deeply that something is kept quiet and you can't see why. But your opinion is irrelevant. They may be right or they may be wrong, and either way your view doesn't come into it. You are trustworthy, and only people who never spread gossip and rumour can be relied on. Who wants a friend who makes their own decisions on which of your confidences to pass on?

I hope I've made my point now, but I'll add one more thing. The way to keep a secret to yourself is not to let anyone know you have it. Once you start saying, 'I know a thing or two, but I'm not supposed to tell you . . .', you have already betrayed the trust of the person who gave you the secret.

RULE 30
Know how to keep a secret

"Face your fears"

Most of us have a few demons in our heads. Some of us have a whole army of them. They lie in wait to ambush you, and then they talk at you, on and on, about things that are bad or scary or sad. They make you worry and panic. That's what they thrive on, those little demons – fear and panic are what they feed on. They have to make you feel bad in order to survive.

You try to shut your ears but it doesn't work – they're inside your head. You tell them to go away but that just makes them cackle more gleefully. There are no weapons to use against them.

Except one. The one thing that makes them scurry back into the corners, and skulk away into the darkest, deepest pits, is a positive happy thought. They can't fight those.

Of course, summoning up cheerful thoughts and images isn't easy when you're defending your sanity against a horde of demons. Which is why you need to be armed and ready at all times. If you have demons living inside your head, design your own comforting, reassuring thoughts to beat them off with. Most of us have some kind of happy place we can go to – designing a dream house, remembering a wonderful occasion, planning an imaginary date – I don't care, so long as it works for you. Sometimes just a distraction that actively engages your brain is sufficient. It just needs to be something that takes a certain degree of attention. That helps to make sure the demons can't sneak in round the back when you're not looking.

Your demons probably come out to attack at predictable times: two in the morning, when you're overworked, just before you visit your mother . . . So these are the times to have your positive images primed and ready to go. You can change your happy thought – or distraction – as often as you like, so long as you always have at least one ready to deploy. Don't relinquish it until the next one is ready for action.

The more effectively you beat off the demon assaults, the more you weaken the demons. Naturally. They're not that smart – they come out because they've always come out at that time of day, or when the terrain is looking rocky. If you can keep them at bay, they probably won't change tactics and creep up on you at other times. But if they do, you're ready for them.

Eventually, if you can force yourself not to give in to them but to face them with happy thoughts, they'll diminish and leave you alone. Some people need professional help to boost their defences, and that's fine. Some people never quite get rid of every last demon, but they reduce the onslaught to a manageable level. And some people manage to see the back of them for good.

RULE 31

Replace the bad thoughts

"Make a New Year's resolution every year"

I was a smoker for many years, and tried several times to give up. I once managed it for eight months, but eventually gave in to its temptations again. Every time I gave up I would plan it, I'd decide when I was going to have my last fag (on New Year's Eve more than once), and I'd savour every drag of that final cigarette before giving up. Within days – hours even – I'd be back at it again, unable to bring myself to stop for good.

One evening in 2002, while sitting watching TV and smoking, a programme came on that changed my attitude completely. Half way through my cigarette I suddenly decided that I didn't want to be a smoker any more.* I stubbed the thing out half smoked, and have never had another one since. I've been tempted, sure, but never irresistibly.

The fact is that on this occasion, for the first time, I actually wanted to stop. I didn't just feel I 'ought' to – I really wanted it. And I realized that actually, whether it's smoking, losing weight, exercising more, or anything else, the important thing is finding a strong enough motivation to carry the resolution through. You can't just wish you wanted to do it, you need to truly want to. Otherwise it's only a matter of time before you go back to your old ways.

That motivation can be wildly different from one person to the next. Some people can watch their closest relatives die of a smoking-related illness and still not give up. You can't buy motivation off the peg – you have to find your own. One of my brothers gave up because he had a 24-hour flight to Australia ahead of him and

---

* No, I'm not telling you what it was – it doesn't matter, it was my motivation, not yours.

knew that, if he was a smoker, he'd never cope. So he had to be a non-smoker before he got on the plane.

I doubt the TV programme that caused me to quit would motivate anyone else (look, it was about parasites if you must know), but that's exactly it: motivation is a very personal thing. The point is that once you find your own motivation you will by definition want to act on it, whenever it happens. Whereas if you try to achieve something you feel you 'should' without the motivation – at New Year or at any other time – it will only fizzle out sooner or later.

Just remember this, next time you are bemoaning the fact that you can't stop biting your nails or start being on time – could it be that you don't really want it enough?

RULE 32

You can't change habits unless you want to

"Respect the elderly"

I can clearly remember being told, when I was a boy, to 'respect the elderly'. I couldn't see why, to be honest, except because I was likely to get a belt round the ear if I didn't. Old people seemed to me to be out of touch, inflexible and in many cases cantankerous old stick-in-the-muds.

Looking back, I think a lot of the problem was that expression, 'the elderly'. It bundled everyone over the age of, oh, I should say around 40 from my childish perspective, into one homogeneous mass. One grey-haired, humbug-sucking, whingeing collective of people, all burbling on about how it wasn't like this in their day.

Of course I didn't include my grandparents in this. I knew them personally, and they weren't like that. They shared a few minor traits with my elderly archetype, but they were far more three-dimensional. Much more interesting altogether.

Now, I'm sorry to say, I'm well on my way to being elderly myself. And apart from the grey hairs, I don't recognize that stereotype in myself at all. Or in any of my friends. Or in the contemporaries I meet. Actually, the more people I encounter, the more I realize that no one fits my stereotype of an elderly person – at least not once I get to know them.

I understand now that the enjoinder to 'respect the elderly' was all wrong. Because despite appearing to be morally righteous, it in fact suggested that all older people were exactly the same, and could be conveniently grouped together in a way which was actually patronizing and dismissive.

The fact is that we should respect everyone, unless they give us a good reason not to. That includes individuals who happen to be old, young or anywhere in between. Or indeed from any background whatever. Everyone is interesting and unique once you scratch deeply enough, and until you have a chance to do so, everyone should be treated with courtesy and consideration.

Yes, indeed, some old people are out of touch. So are some young people. Meanwhile, many older people have an enviable grasp of new technology and can find their way around Facebook in the dark.* Some of them dislike change, and many of them always did, even when they were nippers. Others love variety and many fall somewhere between the extremes. Some older people have been through a lot and learnt nothing, and others have used their time well and are extremely wise. Maybe they always were, even when they were young.

If anyone respects me 20 years from now, I don't want them to do it because I'm grey-haired and suck humbugs all day long. I want them to do it because I'm me.

RULE 33
Respect everyone

---

* I know, it's never really dark on Facebook.

"Look after number one"

In a way, I don't advocate breaking this Rule. But I don't interpret it in the way it's generally meant. The usual implication is that you should focus on your own needs and sod everyone else. In fact, like some looking-glass world, I've found that you need to put your own wishes on one side if you want to feel really good.

It took one of my children to bring this Rule into perspective. He came home from school one evening at the age of about 12 and said he'd had a great day. He'd helped out a friend who was having problems of some kind, and listened to another one who wanted to get frustrations off his chest. Then he'd noticed that one of the office staff was struggling to shift some stuff so he mucked in and helped. He told me he'd had a brilliant day because, in his words, 'I like helping other people. It makes me feel good about myself'.

Like a blinding flash, I realized that he had put into a nutshell what I'd spent years failing to express so clearly. Somehow his phrasing was so simple that everything fell into place. I'd long since noticed that people who are always helping others seem to be the most content. The final Rule of my book *The Rules of Love* is 'Other people are where it's at'. My son, however, had identified the link between helping others and how it affects your self-image.

It's difficult to emphasize how important this Rule is to a happy life. When you help other people it does indeed give you a strong and positive self-image, which in turn builds your confidence. It takes your mind off your own problems, and it means you like yourself more. It's the nearest thing I know to a psychological cure-all.

It really doesn't seem to matter whether you focus your efforts on your own family or on distant people you've never met. You can dedicate your life to charity, or spend it looking after your kids.

You can do the weekly shopping for your neighbour, devote a day a week to the local charity, become a full-time doctor, or just keep an eye out for everyday opportunities to be of help. Obviously you need to be consistent to get those good feelings – it's no good working with dedication for a charity six days a week, and then kicking old ladies you pass in the street on the way home. You need to put helping other people first all the time.

That doesn't mean, however, that you should have no time for yourself. You don't have to go out looking for people to help at all hours of the day and night. Don't worry, you can still have evenings with your feet up in front of the TV. You can have fun, go on holiday, have nights out with friends. You don't have to change your life (unless you want to). It's an outlook, an attitude, a default setting. Help out wherever you see it's needed, before you consider yourself, and you'll unexpectedly find that 'number one' seems to be quite content thank you.

RULE 34
Helping other people makes you feel good about yourself

"If you're in the firing line, keep your head down"

There are people in the world who will try to get the better of you. I've no idea why they do it – they all have their own reasons, none of which constitutes a decent excuse. But it happens. They put you down, they show you up, they grind away at your self-esteem, they bully you. Some single you out, others do it to almost everyone. It's generally worst in schools, and reduces through life as other people mature, and as your own resilience increases. But from time to time you can encounter it at any stage in life.

The question is, how are you going to deal with it? Are you going to believe what they say about you, allow your self-confidence and self-esteem to slowly leach away until you feel worthless? That's often what happens, and it's quite understandable why these people have this effect. But it's not the result you want. You want to prevent them from denting your self-image. You want their put-downs and bullying to slide off you.

I wish I could give you a couple of Rules that would instantly cure all bullying. Wouldn't that be great? Of course it's not that simple. However, I can pass on a few of the tips that have worked for other people. If you're pretty robust, and fairly confident, and the bully isn't a dominant force in your life, they may work on their own. If, on the other hand, you're really up against it, they'll certainly help but it will take longer, and you may need extra outside help. There are great books out there, and expert counsellors.

The thing you need to know, whether you're being bullied at school or in your retirement home, is that the problem is theirs and not yours. There is never any excuse for picking on people, regardless of their behaviour, and your bully is never right or justified or excused. The issue for you is to try to detach yourself emotionally and refuse to let them get to you. Much easier said than done, I realize.

One thing that has helped several people I know is a simple phrase to repeat to yourself in times of trouble: they can't walk all over you unless you're lying down. So if you refuse to take it – whether overtly by standing up to them, or whether just privately inside your head – you'll protect yourself. There are lots of techniques for dealing with bullies, but this is a great personal defence, before you even start on specific strategies. If you keep telling yourself this, you feel that you're not letting them through, that you have an invisible force field that all their barbs simply bounce off. It makes no difference whether they know they're losing or not. What matters is that *you* know *you're* not.

RULE 35

They can't walk all over you unless you're lying down

"Just ignore the bullies"

Listen, I'm no expert and I'm not about to set myself up as one. If you have a big problem with being bullied, try to find yourself someone who really knows what they're talking about. What I can do is pass on a few tips, and some strategies that I've observed working for other people. But don't let anyone who isn't an expert – myself included – tell you what you should do. Some techniques work brilliantly for some people and not for others. So these are some ideas to try if you feel comfortable, and not if you don't.

My first suggestion is that you ignore anyone who tells you to just ignore bullying. Sometimes it works, more often it doesn't. But crucially it implies that it's your fault, and if you only responded the right way it would all stop, so you have only yourself to blame. Wrong, wrong, wrong! The ball is not in your court. You shouldn't be having to deal with this at all, in any fashion.

Nevertheless, you probably want to deal with it if you can, so here are some thoughts. First, if you can, talk to someone in authority who can intervene for you. A manager, teacher or whoever. They need to know, and many people who think that their boss can't help are subsequently surprised to find that they can. It's extremely unlikely to make things any worse, so what can you lose?

I know one teenager who says that her favourite way to wrong-foot people who pick on her is to agree with them. One of my favourite phrases for this is to say, 'I should think you're probably right'. You're not actually saying they *are* right, but it sounds as if you are. My teenage friend advises that you agree with them brightly, rather than sounding resigned and downtrodden. She also says it's important that you don't actually convince yourself they're right, so either don't actually listen to them, or cross your fingers, or in some way signal to yourself that you don't believe what you're telling them.*

---

* Yes, I am advocating lying. But only in self-defence.

Another ploy is to ask them a direct question, preferably in the company of people they don't want to lose face in front of. Be calm and reasonable, and assertive. Keep the moral high ground and don't accuse them of anything – just state facts. So you might ask a colleague at a meeting, 'Why do you often say I'm rubbish at my job, when I exceeded my targets last year?' Don't let them off the hook if they laugh it off or don't answer the question, and be ready to back up your statements. So if they deny having said it, you can say, 'On Monday when we were at your desk discussing the new software system, you said . . .' Just repeat the question until you get a satisfactory answer. The idea is that if you make them feel uncomfortable for bullying you, it will be easier for them to stop.

Rule 34, as I'm sure you remember, was about how helping other people increases your self-esteem. This is a great way to counteract its erosion by bullies. Find an opportunity to make a difference to someone who will value you. That will make it much harder for the bully to affect you.

RULE 36
Don't let 'em bully you

"Think on your feet"

In some situations, thinking on your feet can work well. Sometimes there's no choice, of course. And some of us find it easier than others. But in tricky situations, it's much smarter to plan in advance what you'll say or how you'll act.

This applies to bullying, just to give you one example, as we've just been thinking about it. If you know that a certain classmate or colleague or 'friend' is likely to make fun of your weight, or your background, or your handwriting, or your sales record, or your hairstyle, or anything else, just decide in advance what you'll say in response. It doesn't have to matter (within reason) what this is. The point is that you're writing the script, which puts you in control. And that has to feel more positive than being a victim.

Here's another example. If you're shy, it can be easy to get anxious about meeting people. Should you shake hands? Maybe kiss? One cheek or both cheeks? What if you start to shake hands and they go in for a kiss? You've no idea what they're going to do, so it's pretty nerve-wracking waiting to see what will happen. But wait – it doesn't have to be like that. Why don't *you* write the script, and then you can control what happens? Decide beforehand that you'll offer your hand, or that you'll grasp them firmly by the shoulders and kiss one cheek, or whatever. If necessary ask advice on what will be appropriate, but the chances are if you're not sure what will happen it's because either option would be acceptable. If in doubt, go for the more formal option.

Whether you're about to ask someone out for the first time, or have to discipline a member of your team, or want to ask your boss for a pay rise, or your tutor for an extension on your assignment, decide in advance how you're going to handle it and, whatever happens, you'll be more confident because you'll be in control.

Obviously these examples are all conversations that could go off in different directions. But you must know roughly what the possibilities are, so you can plan contingencies: if she says no, you'll say this; if she says yes, you'll say that, and so on.

The real value of this isn't in knowing whether to kiss or shake hands, or in being able to cope with bullies, or take a knock-back when you're asking for a date. It's the confidence you gain from feeling that you're in control.

RULE 37
Be in control

"What you do is more important than why you do it"

You can fool most of the people most of the time. In fact you can fool some of the people all of the time. But there's one person you should never fool, and that's yourself. It may sound obvious, but it's harder than you think.

Sometimes we pretend to do things for one reason, when our real motive is different. It could be that we're ashamed or embarrassed by our real aim. Perhaps we make out we want to score goals so the team can win, but secretly we just want to score more than a particular rival within our own team. That doesn't sound so good, does it? So we stick to the 'all for the team's benefit' story.

Or maybe we decide to stay in our job because we enjoy the social circle we have there. But we want to come across as being more ambitious than that, so we pretend it's because the promotion prospects are good, or the job is more secure. Perhaps we come to believe that ourselves.

When I was 16 I told my mum I'd decided to leave school before the end of the year and get a job. I felt it was important I get started on the work ladder, and it was time I brought some income into the house. She was quite impressed. Actually, though, I only quit because I'd got wind that they were about to expel me. But I didn't think she needed to know that.

Some of these things are important and some aren't. Sometimes the truth is pretty close to the story we're telling, and sometimes it's a long way off. It may or may not matter that we're not being honest with other people – that's for other Rules to cover. But you should never, never talk yourself into believing the fiction.

No matter how close it is to the truth, no matter that there's some truth in both versions, no matter what.

However embarrassing or shameful or demeaning or low your real motives, you must always be brutal with yourself. Deep down you have to say, 'Who am I kidding? I just want to get one over on so-and-so . . .', or 'Well, that's partly why I want to do it. But actually the real reason is . . .'

And why must you do this? You must do it because if you don't, you'll lose track of yourself. You have to know who you are, and it's your motives that reveal this more than anything. Once you start fooling yourself, you stop being able to judge your own behaviour, to monitor whether you're behaving as you should – as you would like to – you lose your moral compass. I'm not talking about whether your motives are right or wrong, whether you're playing by the Rules or not. You could have the best of motives, and your actions could be exemplary. But that doesn't change the fact that you will lose your way unless, somewhere in your heart, you acknowledge the truth, if only to yourself.

RULE 38

Be honest
with yourself

"You can judge a book by its cover"

Can you imagine how different you'd be if you'd grown up differently? Suppose your parents had been much poorer, or much wealthier, than they were. Suppose you'd gone to a very different school. Perhaps the people around you might have all had very different values and beliefs. Suppose you'd suffered a dreadful bereavement as a child (or that you hadn't . . .). Maybe you'd grown up with a serious disability (or without one . . .). What if you'd had lots of siblings, or none at all? Lived in a war zone, or miles from anywhere, or moved around every few months, or lived in care homes?

These things shape us, and there's not a lot we can do about it. Once we're adults, we can make a choice to live a decent life, to live by the Rules, but we'll still be deeply influenced by what we've been through.

And that's not only true of you and me. It's true of everyone we meet, work with, make friends with, pass in the street. That barista who just served you coffee, your boss's husband, the garage mechanic, your child's schoolteacher, your next-door neighbour, they all walked a completely unique path to get to where they are now. And pretty well every one of them has some bad bits in their past – as well as lots of good stuff, I hope. Actually some people have precious little good stuff.

People come in and out of our own lives, often momentarily, and it's easy to be lulled into feeling that they only exist while they're crossing our path. For us, that's true in a sense. But then we only exist as a brief flash for them. In fact everyone has a completely original and personal story, and all the chapters of that story shape the person they are. If we don't know that whole story, how can we judge the person? Perhaps they are the way they are because of some great trauma in their past, or a deep grief, or a sense of loss, or a frustration they can never satisfy.

So next time someone winds you up, or irritates you, or strikes you as being weak or arrogant or foolish or pompous or selfish or over-competitive or inhibited or pushy, just remember that you have no idea by what route they got here, and maybe they've been through things that you can't imagine.

Yes, we're all responsible for our own actions. Yes, there's no excuse for certain kinds of behaviour – those that negatively affect other people – but that's a much bigger ask of some people than of others, and we can't know what each person's story is. Perhaps they have no excuse for being selfish, thoughtless, unkind, intolerant, aggressive. Or perhaps they have no idea that's how they appear, or have no understanding that these are bad things, or perhaps they are even doing their best to change but have the odds stacked against them.

For us, as Rules players, that means we need to stop, think, and be more tolerant. Better to be forgiving to someone who doesn't deserve it than to judge someone who deserves a break.

RULE 39
Everyone has a backstory

"Put the past behind you"

You may have been through some tough times in your life. Maybe some terrible times.

A lot of people will tell you that once you become a grown-up, you need to put the past – or at least the bad bits of it – in a box and close the lid on it. It can't be changed, and now you need to get on with the rest of your life. They're not being unsympathetic, these people, they just want to help you. And they think that if you dwell on your past it will hamper you. So they advise the old-fashioned, stiff upper-lip approach.

Well, it doesn't work.

You can put stuff in a box alright – some people find this harder than others; some find it very easy. Yes, you can close the lid too. What you can't do, however, is put the box down and walk away. That's just not how it works. Nor are you allowed to give it away – it's your box and yours alone. What you'll have to do is carry that box around with you *forever*. It's a heavy box, even on a good day. And there will be times when the stuff inside the box lies quietly, and other times when it bangs on the lid and keeps you awake at night.

Sure, there are lots of bad bits of our childhoods that can go in the box and they weigh very little and will probably never disturb our dreams again. But the really big stuff, the stuff that shaped the person you've become, you can't shut that away because – for better or worse – it's a part of you.

If you have this kind of stuff, you'll have to deal with it. Sooner or later, you'll have to come to terms with it. You might wait years, or do it now. You might make some headway and then take a break before you go back to it. You might do it alone, or with a friend, or a psychotherapist, or a counsellor, or through meditation. There are lots of options. In the end, though, it's all about recognizing that however bad that stuff was, it's what made you the fabulous person you are today, so you need to end up at least on nodding terms with it.

Once you've done that, obviously you can't leave it behind (because, as we've said, it's part of you), but you can put it in the box and it won't weigh nearly as much. And occasionally you can even take it out of the box for a bit, and that will be OK too. *Then* you can get on with the rest of your life.

RULE 40

You have to deal with your stuff before you can get on with your life

---

"What about me?"

You see the world from your own perspective – of course you do. What can be harder to recognize is that not everyone else does. When you're a little kid, most of the people in your world are focused on you a lot of the time. But when you grow up, you have to recognize that this stops being true. Otherwise you'll become selfish and self-centred and no fun to be around.

When you're 2, you can scream when you're hungry and someone will produce food for you. It's not going to work when you're 20. OK, so you'd worked that one out already. But there are other ways in which we can all too easily assume that the world is focused on us, when in fact no one else is giving us a thought.

I heard a kid at the school gates the other day – he must have been about 12 or 13 – moaning at his mum and saying, 'But *why* did Mr Stone decide not to put me in the football team?' Just think about that question for a minute. It assumes that Mr Stone was focused on deciding what to do with little Johnny, and opted to exclude him from the team. Actually, I very much doubt that's what was going through his head. Far more likely that he considered who the best 11 players in the year were, and Johnny's name wasn't on the list. Although Johnny's world revolves around Johnny, Mr Stone's doesn't.

This is an easy trap to fall into right through life, especially if we had parents who put us at the centre of their world. Part of growing up is recognizing that other people might not have us in mind at all, and accepting that that's right and normal. After all, we aren't thinking of everyone who is affected every time we make a decision. Suppose you arrange to meet with a group of friends at 8pm. If there are several of you and one person can't make it that late, you're not trying to exclude them, you simply can't fit around everyone and they're the unlucky one who missed out this time.

In the same way, if you're the one who can't make it, it's not because everyone is ganging up on you. It's just that there's no time that suits everyone. Get over it.

So if someone's forgotten you're vegetarian, or you've missed out on promotion, or your dad forgot to ask if you're feeling better after that bout of illness, or someone else is getting the attention, or the landlord has given you notice, don't feel aggrieved or offended. Just accept that it's the way the world works. Everyone has a load of other stuff on their minds, and they're assuming that you'll respond in the same grown-up fashion as everyone else.

I may sound a bit shirty, because adults who expect the world to revolve around them are pretty irritating. But I'm actually telling you this because once you recognize that it's not about you, it means that no one is trying to offend you or disrespect you or slight you. And that should make it much easier to respond equably.

RULE 41

It's not all about you

"Just once won't hurt"

I remember when I first started smoking. I was 6. My mother used to get us kids to light her fags for her from the gas cooker in the kitchen.* The only way to get them going properly was to take a drag on them. By the time I was 8 I was stealing cigarettes from my mother. At 10, I was 'borrowing' money from her to buy my own. It crept up on me insidiously, years before I had any idea smoking was bad for you, and it took me decades to kick the habit. Quitting was much tougher than not starting would have been all those years ago.

It's so easy to tell yourself you're not going to make a habit of drinking, or eating badly, or cutting the time too fine to get to work, or having a glass of brandy before bed (there's a trap I fell into when I gave up the cigarettes – out of the frying pan, etc.). But the easiest time to quit any bad habit is before you start. If you can't give up the first drink, doughnut or whatever, you'll never have it so easy again.

Look, I'm telling you this because I've learnt the hard way, not because I'm some virtuous goody-goody who wouldn't know a bad habit if it ran slap bang into them. I've fallen into so many bad ways over the years – and eventually clawed my way back out of most of them. And every time I've wished I'd never started.

I have got better though, as the years have gone by. The trick is to recognize the potential habit before it's fully formed. That way you can take avoiding action. For example, it's very tempting when filling up the car at the petrol station to buy a bar of chocolate or a bag of crisps when you pay. Obviously it's a popular habit, or the petrol stations wouldn't have shelves full of the stuff next to the till. When I was young, the attendant filled the car up for you

---

* Yes, I know this sounds ridiculous. But it was the 1950s, and people weren't aware of how dangerous smoking was. Or at least my mother wasn't.

and you never got out. They didn't sell snacks. Once fuel stations started popping up where you filled the car up yourself and then went into a shop to pay, I did actually realize right from the start how sorry I would be if I ever bought a snack. I might think it was 'just once' but I'd be on a slippery slope. I'm now entirely in the habit of paying for my fuel and getting out fast before the chocolate bars catch my eye – but I know how fast that habit could change if I succumbed even once.

Running late. There's another habit it's easy to fall into. Once you discover how forgiving people usually are when you turn up 5 minutes late, it's easy to stop making such an effort to be on time. Before you know it, you're keeping people waiting 10 or 15 minutes. That's downright unfair and disrespectful and you know it, and you'll definitely stop doing it . . . next time. You see how hard it is to break the habit? So take my advice and don't start.

RULE 42

Don't let bad habits get a foot in the door

"Be spontaneous"

Let me tell you a story about someone who contacted me after reading *The Rules of Life*. He sent me a private letter via my publisher so no one else could read what he had to say. Apparently he found *The Rules of Life* in an airport bookshop and decided to buy it. But there was a very long queue so, on the spur of the moment, he decided to walk out without paying for it. He'd never done anything like that before, and couldn't say what had prompted him to break the law.

He felt guilty for a few moments, and then put it out of his mind. However, once on the plane he started reading the book and encountered a number of Rules that made him feel dreadfully guilty. From Rule 3 onwards the guilt started to grow, and by Rule 33 he was abject. He realized he'd let himself down badly, and had really messed up.

He could have kept quiet and put it down to experience, but he didn't feel right just leaving it alone. So he decided to make up for it as best he could. He sent me a letter of apology explaining what he'd done, which I have to say I found immensely entertaining given the irony of having picked that particular book to make off with. He also sent me a £50 note to compensate for having stolen the book.* And he bought and paid for three more copies to give to friends. He even 'fessed up to his wife, despite knowing that she would verbally shred him for doing such a thing.

And he very kindly gave me his own Rule that he'd learnt from this, which I'm now passing on to you. Deep down he knew at the time that what he was doing was wrong. His conscience, his heart, was telling him so. A little voice tried to warn him but he didn't listen to it. So his Rule was that you should always listen to that little voice, because you'll regret it if you don't.

---

* I gave this to charity as it was way more than I'd normally earn for a single copy, and I didn't want to inherit his guilt.

He also made sure that when he did acknowledge his error, he did everything he could to put it right. If you don't listen to that voice before you've gone wrong, the next best thing is to listen to it afterwards and make amends as well as possible. And, as this particular reader shows, it's never too late to listen. As a result of his belated honesty, he learnt a useful lesson, gave me a great Rule to share with anyone who wants it, donated £50 to charity, bought three books, and provided me with one of the most interesting pieces of correspondence I've ever read.

RULE 43

Listen to the voices in your head

"Take one step at a time"

If you're trying to write a book, as I've learnt over the years, the prospect can be daunting. So the best approach is to tackle it in small chunks. One chapter at a time (or in my case, one Rule). 'Eat an elephant one bite at a time', as they say. That works for writing reports or dissertations too. And it works for renovating a car or refurbishing a house. Little by little is an effective approach to most practical projects.

However, if you want to make major changes to your life, it's not the way to go about it. Sure, you can tweak the smaller dissatisfactions to make modest improvements, but for the big stuff, you can't pussyfoot around. You have to jump.

Suppose, for example, that you're not happy with your weight. If you want to lose a few pounds, you can adjust your diet to shave off a few calories here and there, and you should achieve your new weight quite easily. But if you want to lose a couple of stone or more – and keep it off – you're going to have to rethink your long-term diet completely. You can't simply skip the odd snack. You'll need to cut out bread and potatoes, eat massively more fruit and vegetables, and keep firmly away from fast food outlets. Your shopping habits will have to change, and the inside of your fridge will look like, well, the inside of someone else's fridge. Not just while the weight is coming off, but for good if you want it to stay off.

Suppose you don't like your job. You could apply for a transfer, or move to another company. But what if you realize you're unhappy with your career? Maybe you've realized you don't want to be an accountant any more. Your passion – you now realize – is to be a tree surgeon. If you really want to succeed in this, you'll need to adapt to a new working regime, a very different salary level, a new diet (you can't support an active, outdoorsy tree surgeon on a sedentary desk worker's diet), and quite possibly a new social life as well. The move isn't going to work unless you embrace it wholeheartedly, and welcome the changes it brings.

An old friend of mine had an office job in London. She was generally dissatisfied with her life and felt she was going nowhere. She'd always had the idea of living in the country rather than the city, but never found an opportunity. So she made her own opportunity. She gave in her notice, found herself a cottage in a little country village, and started up her own business. Now some people might think that changing so many things at once was foolhardy. But she succeeded largely because she had thrown everything up in the air and made a fresh start.

Another friend found that none of his relationships lasted more than a couple of years. Eventually, after one more failure, he recognized that he was putting his work before his partner every time. So he changed to a related but less stressful job, and booked some counselling sessions. He soon met a lovely woman and this time he approached his life from the other direction entirely. He put the relationship first, and really worked at it. It felt very different, but it eventually became habit and several years on they're still very happily together.

I've known people move abroad, end relationships, change careers, take a massive salary drop – and I've observed that these big changes, so long as they're well thought through, seem to work far more often than trying to effect big change without doing things very differently.

RULE 44
If you want big things to change, you have to make big changes

---

"The best people will be there for you for life"

Ah, if only this were true. The best people may indeed be with you for life – but it could be their life and not yours. The fact is that people die. Some of us learn this brutally as children, many of us are relatively sheltered from it until we get older. Perhaps as children we lose the odd grandparent when their time is up. But sooner or later, we'll lose people who are really close – parents, siblings, best friends, even our own children.

I'm telling you this because if you haven't yet discovered it for yourself, it will come as a horrible shock. Even though of course you know it intellectually, the reality is worse than you can imagine. And it will keep happening, all through your life. There will be lulls, and there will also be years when you feel people are dying all around you. And it won't get any easier to cope with. You may become more attuned to the general idea of it, but each person is precious in themselves, and no easier to say goodbye to for having done it so many times before.

It's other people's deaths that give us a sense of our own mortality. It's hard to believe in your own death, especially when you're young. As people around you die, you start to realize that one day it will be your turn.

But there's one thing that makes all this alright. Yes, really, it is OK. Because new people come along, and they take the place of the people who have gone. I don't mean they replace them, but they occupy a space the same size in our hearts. So as we go through life, we should aim to make room for at least as many new people as there are those who have gone. I never really understood this until I had children of my own. Then I realized that if life stood still, my grandparents, parents and old friends might still be alive, but I'd be missing out on so much – without knowing it – that it wouldn't be worth it.

Of course some individual deaths are never OK, especially those who die young, or those whose deaths affect the very young. But the principle of people dying is worth having if it means that new people are born. You don't have to have your own children for this to make sense – other people's children can bring huge joy into your life (and be a lot less work).

My grandmother had a favourite poem, *The Middle* by Ogden Nash, which she used to recite, and which sums up my point pretty well:

When I remember bygone days
I think how evening follows morn;
So many I loved were not yet dead,
So many I love were not yet born.

RULE 45

People come and go, and it's OK

"Enjoy yourself while you're young"

Here's a Rule that you don't have to break in every sense. Everyone should enjoy themselves as much as they can – without hurting other people – whatever age they are. However, I've included it here because I want to emphasize that there are limits, especially when it comes to your body.

You can throw a lot at your body when you're young – drink, drugs, late nights, wild escapades. And you'll probably get away with it . . . for a while. I came off my motorbike when I was 16 and smashed up my knee. It recovered in a way I really had no right to expect, because it was only a 16-year-old knee, although it was never quite the same again. But once I was in my forties, it started giving me serious gyp. When you're 16, it's hard to care much about what will happen when you're 40 – it's too far off. But when you're 40 with a painful knee you're horribly aware of how long you could have to live with it.

I put my body through a lot of stuff as a teenager that I've regretted since. Actually I regretted some of it at the time, but everyone else was doing it and I didn't have the sense then to follow my own judgement. So I'm not going to be such a hypocrite as to tell anyone else that they shouldn't do it. You can do what you like. I'm just letting you know that the day may come when you wish you'd eased off a bit. Or in some cases not done it at all (I'm thinking hard drugs here).

I'm not lecturing you about what you ought to do. But the day may come when you regret some of the wilder moments of your youth. So be a bit smart about looking ahead to whether your behaviour now might have long-term consequences. When you're young you think you'll live for ever, *carpe diem* and all that. But there is a later, and if you ignore it now, you may be sorry when you reach it.

Look at how professional footballers and sportspeople retire, or at least step down from international sport, somewhere in their early thirties usually. That's because even they, with all their fitness training and exercise, just can't get as much out of their bodies once they pass about 30. The body simply isn't designed for it.

By all means use your body, work it, and give it a bit of punishment too if it can take it. But avoid excesses, and don't ignore the minor gripes and problems.

I don't suggest for a moment that you should avoid all fun. There's no point living to a ripe old age if you're going to do that. But listen, if you want to enjoy the last half or two-thirds of your life as much as the first stretch, just look after your body properly. It may sound boring and middle-aged but, believe me, once you *are* middle-aged it won't seem boring.

RULE 46
Your body is for life

"Borrowing is OK so long as you can pay it back"

This is a very specific manifestation of the 'Let's worry about that another day' principle. And this is a very expensive version. It's true that you can always find money if you're desperate. Trouble is, the more desperate you are, the more it will cost you. The whole point about loans – from banks, venture capitalists, loan sharks, credit cards or anyone else – is that they make money out of lending to you because you pay interest. That means that you end up having to pay back even more, and if you haven't got the money now, how are you going to repay even more than you've gained by borrowing? The more desperate you are, the harder it becomes to find a legitimate lender, and the more likely that you'll have to resort to a less scrupulous source, which will cost you even more. So don't do it.

If you can't afford whatever it is – a car, furniture, clothes, evenings out, a holiday – then go without until you can afford it. Trust me, the short-term benefits won't be worth the spiralling misery of debt. And debt always spirals – the interest grows, you have to borrow more to pay off the original debt, you need another loan because it's getting harder to cover your everyday costs. And that horrible sinking in the pit of your stomach just gets worse every time. You will so regret buying that car, or taking that holiday, or having such a fancy wedding.

Of course, not everyone who takes out a loan ends up in debtors' gaol. But even if you do successfully pay it back, it still costs you money. When it's all paid back, you have less than you'd have if you hadn't borrowed in the first place. So it just makes no sense.

However tough things are, don't borrow money unless you genuinely can't eat or have no roof over your head.

Speaking of a roof over your head, I will make an exception here for mortgages. If you can afford to buy a house without a mortgage, go for it. But not many of us are in that position. In which case you might as well pay your monthly living expenses to a mortgage company and end up with a house at the end of it, than pay it to a landlord and end up with nothing. Just don't take out a bigger mortgage than you can afford, mind.

You may be thinking that you could borrow money from family or friends. Well, maybe you could. But if things go wrong – possibly even if they don't – you could find yourself sacrificing friendships and family relationships. It just isn't worth it. And however sure you are that things won't go wrong, you can never be certain. Suppose you have an accident and can't work? Even in the best case, it sets up an unequal relationship where you don't want one. How can you look your sister or dad or best mate in the eye when you owe them £500 or even £5k – let alone when you fail to repay it on time? They're there to pick you up emotionally when times get tough, not to bail you out financially. They can't necessarily do both.

If you're lucky enough to have parents who give you money from time to time, especially while you're getting started in life, that's different. If there are no strings, and it comes from the heart. But don't accept any form of loan that needs to be repaid.

RULE 47
Don't get into debt

"Be generous"

By all means be generous with your time, your skills, your love and your hospitality, even your money (sometimes), but there is one respect in which you should never ever be generous. Loans and friendships don't mix. And that works both ways. If you lend one of your family or friends a lot of money and they fail to repay it, what will that do to the relationship? I've known people abandon their friends and go AWOL because they were ashamed that they couldn't repay them. Do you want to lose the money and the friend? It's happened to me. It's even more uncomfortable with family. How are you going to get through Christmas at your parents' house when your brother still hasn't returned the money he promised to repay you in the summer?

Of course friends and family don't just stop at money. Oh no. They want to borrow your car, your laptop, stay in your house when you're on holiday. And suppose they damage the car, break the laptop, trash the house? You may well trust them not to do it on purpose, but accidents happen. What if they can't afford to repair the damage or replace the computer? Anyway, even if they can replace things, that's not necessarily what you want – you want those files from your computer, or that vase your grandmother left you that's in pieces since they knocked it over.

So what can you do? Just tell them to push off? That's not very friendly either. If it's a big thing they're asking, it's completely reasonable and they'll understand. But if it's a relatively small loan (to you), or the use of something that's precious to you, you might feel you want to say yes. But how can you avoid the risk to the relationship?

There's a simple acid test here. Would you be prepared to write off the loan if you had to? Is the friendship worth more than that? If so, you can carry on and lend them the money (or the laptop or whatever) and tell yourself it's a gift. If they want to call it a loan, that's up to them. And if you get the money back eventually, that will be a nice bonus. But write it off in your head, so that your relationship won't be damaged if you never see the money again, or if you come home to a house that's a mess.

Good friends and family will understand if you choose to say no to a loan. You can explain that if anything happened to stop them repaying it, you feel it would destroy the relationship and you value them too much for that. If they can't understand that, and still put you under pressure, you might want to ask yourself how good a friend they really are if they can't respect your view.

I can't tell you how liberating this approach is. Since I discovered it many years ago (from a close friend) it has made the business of lending things to friends so much simpler. The second I've handed over the dosh, I don't give it another thought. That feels good – because I don't do it unless I can afford to. And boy, is it enjoyable getting back money that I'd entirely forgotten lending.

RULE 48
Never lend money unless you're prepared to write it off

"Believe you're the best"

In one of my previous incarnations I worked with small businesses. I saw lots of businesses thrive and grow, and inevitably I saw plenty fail too. Often you can predict perfectly well who will succeed and who won't.* One thing I found was a pretty good indicator of failure was companies that always dissed their competitors. They were arrogantly convinced that the competition was hopeless, and consequently it always caught them quite off-guard when their competitors ran off with all their customers.

It's not only businesses that fall prey to this attitude. Some people believe they're the best when they simply aren't. Whether you're convinced you're fantastic at your job, or a great parent, or the top student, or a brilliant sportsperson, it's a dangerous attitude.

I'm all for being positive, and for building your self-esteem, but not at the expense of honesty. You have to be truthful with yourself about how good you are. Anyone who is genuinely brilliant at their job will always be looking for ways to get even better – that's one of the requirements for job brilliance – and therefore will accept that they're not perfect. It's always dangerous to give yourself 10 out of 10. Even Usain Bolt is forever trying to shave a few milliseconds off his running time, so I guess he'd give himself just under 10 out of 10. He doesn't strike me as being under-confident or negative in the least – just realistic. He's the best, but he's open to the possibility that he could be better still.

The fact is that as soon as you believe you're the greatest, you become complacent. You stop looking for ways to get even better. Why would you, if you're already at the top of the pile? But in

---

* This isn't a book about business, I know, but I must digress just to tell you the biggest 'we're doomed' line I ever heard from a small business owner: 'The trouble is, we make big pieces of furniture, but people only seem to want to buy small pieces of furniture. What can we do?'

order to improve you need a clear understanding of where you are, combined with a clear vision of where you want to be. Only then can you draw up a realistic plan to get yourself from here to there. If you think you're already there, you've got no chance.

So big yourself up by all means. Tell yourself how good you are and give yourself brownie points, pats on the back and meta-phorical gold stars. Just don't believe your own hype so readily that you lose sight of the truth, because that's a sure-fire route to failure.

RULE 49
Know your real worth

"Don't allow people to make you feel bad"

Don't you hate it when people patronize you, or moan at you, or emotionally blackmail you? In fact, lots of people do even smaller things that really wind you up – they mumble, or leave doors open, or tap their feet incessantly, or hum out of tune when you're trying to concentrate, or always walk out of the room in the middle of a sent . . .

Sorry. I'm back now.* Where was I? Ah yes, people who leave you feeling frustrated, irritated, anxious, depressed, stressed, or otherwise not as you'd like to feel. You really shouldn't let them do it. Why not have a word and get them to change their behaviour, or if necessary aspects of their personality?

I'll tell you why not. Because it won't work, that's why not. Occasionally you might tactfully persuade your partner or your mum to stop phoning during your favourite TV programme, or not to slam your car door, but for the most part you'll get no joy. You'll just create resentment and arguments. And frankly, if everyone you knew kept asking you to change this or that little habit or characteristic, can you honestly say that you'd studiously adapt to all their requests without complaint?

So it's out of your control. Except, hang on a minute, there's one thing that is still within your control. Yep, your own reaction. You might not be able to stop your friends' little habits, or indeed stop strangers from stepping on your toes, or keeping you waiting, or not listening properly to what you're saying. But it is entirely in your control whether you let it get to you, or whether you let it all wash over you.

---

* I have to confess that this is one of my worse habits. Apparently.

This also applies of course to inanimate objects. When your car runs out of petrol (which is never your own fault, obviously), or the internet connection goes down, or it's raining and you're not dressed for it, you can still choose how you react.

I know it's harder to respond cheerfully when it's raining and you're running late than when you're relaxing on a sunny beach, for example. But to be honest, if you can't change your response, you're dooming yourself to frustration and misery, and how will that help? No, if you want to enjoy life as much of the time as possible, you need to take control. That doesn't just mean taking control of your actions, but also taking control of your reactions. You can be inconvenienced and mind, or inconvenienced and not mind. Your call. I know which I'd prefer.

RULE 50
The only thing you can control is you

"Some people just get to you"

You must know certain people who have a habit of making you angry, or upset, or depressed. Even the people who mostly make you feel great can occasionally make you feel bad.

It's a very common expression: 'He makes me so cross', or 'She always makes me feel inadequate', or 'He makes me feel guilty'. So common that almost everyone believes it. But we're not all so malleable that we're just victims – pawns in someone else's game. People can behave in ways that make a certain response seem easier, but you don't have to get stuck in that initial reaction. As you'll see, this is an extension of the previous Rule.

If you don't want to feel a particular way, just don't feel it. I know that's far easier to say than to do, especially after years of forming a habitual response to certain things. Your brain has spent years beating a neural pathway to a certain response, and you'll have to retrain it. But that can be done. Just refuse to listen to your mind telling you that you're guilty or cross or inadequate, and tell it even more firmly that you're at ease or calm or confident or whatever you would prefer to feel.

Suppose your partner 'makes' you angry by shouting at you. Try thinking of it this way: your partner shouted at you and you got angry.

Now take it further: your partner shouted. You got angry.

Now for the next step: your partner did what they did. You did anger.

Well, if you can do anger, you can do something else instead. What would you rather do – calm? OK, then do calm instead. Why should your partner doing whatever it is they did have control over your feelings? We've already established that *you* control your feelings. So just keep telling yourself, 'I'm choosing to do calm'.

There's some neuroscience behind this that I'm not going to bore you with,* and it doesn't matter anyway. The point is that you need to train your mind to ignore the old neural pathway by forging a new one. Keep telling yourself in this situation that you're doing calm – if it helps, visualize feeling calm, or recall a time when you've felt very calm – and before long your brain will get into the habit of following the new pathway whenever your partner shouts at you.

Whatever is getting to you, just tell yourself that it is what it is, or that that person did what they did, or said what they said. Then *choose* which emotion you're going to do, and do it.

RULE 51

No one can make you feel anything

---

* Because I'd probably get the details wrong . . .

"You can't help how you feel"

Once again this is a natural follow-on from the last Rule. There are some feelings that you can most certainly help, as we've just seen. But quite apart from what other people 'make' you feel – or don't – there's a broader principle here.

We all talk to ourselves more than we probably realize. It's not a sign of madness, it's just how people are. Try monitoring your internal conversations for a few days, and listen out objectively for the tone of voice you use.

Some people have conciliatory, forgiving inner voices: 'Never mind, you can't do everything', or 'You may not have found time to call mum, but you managed everything else on today's list'. Others have little slave-drivers in their heads: 'You really should have managed that', or 'Poor mum, it's not fair on her. She'll be feeling abandoned and forgotten and it's all your fault'.

If you spend most of your time being spoken to like this – even by yourself – you'll soon start feeling inadequate and guilty, negative and with low self-esteem. So if you catch yourself doing this, stop and reinvent your inner voice. Start telling yourself how well you're doing (realistically, of course), and cut yourself a bit of slack.

Once again, train yourself to think in positive terms. The moment you catch a negative thought about to form, and before it's put itself into words, overlay it with the thought you'd *like* to have. Keep on doing this and you'll find within a few days – if you're persistent and relentless about it – that your mood lifts. Just as it would if you were on a long journey and swapped a miserable, doom-laden companion for a positive, sunny one. Which is pretty much what's actually happening.

I've seen people with serious psychological disorders turned around by this approach. It's hard work, but not for very long. It soon becomes habit most of the time and you rarely have to adjust your inner voice any more. Sometimes an emotional trauma can set you back a bit, but you have the wherewithal to get back on track.

Our inner voices have a lot to do with our backgrounds. If you've been brought up by critical parents you're likely to have a more critical or negative inner voice than someone who's been brought up by loving and reassuring parents. But the great news is that, with persistence, this strategy will work no matter how you got where you are.

RULE 52

You feel what you think

"Actions speak louder than words"

It's funny how we unconsciously fall into a pattern of behaviour with people. Sometimes different patterns with different people (even though you are fundamentally the same). Things that often vary include how demonstrative you are, how much you share with them, how much you talk about feelings (or not). I guess that explains why there's so much variation in what we say to different people about how much they mean to us.

On one level, if someone knows that you love, care, value and appreciate them, you could argue that it doesn't matter much whether you actually say so. It's only words, and you show them in everything you do how much they mean to you.

Or do you? Some people have such a low opinion of themselves, they don't recognize others' appreciation unless it's spelt out in capital letters right under their nose. Or they can tell you care, but they don't realize how much – they know you like them, but they aren't aware how much their friendship means to you. Actually, unless you tell someone loud and clear how much you value them, they *don't* know.

What's more, it feels really good to have someone who matters to you tell you that they reciprocate your feelings. Why not give someone that pleasure, if you care about them? Your family and friends may not realize just which qualities you treasure in them, so why not hold up a mirror to them and let them see what makes them so special. Tell them that they're a great listener, or you love them for their ability to make you laugh at yourself, or there's no one better when you just need sympathy, or it's wonderful to have a friend who really gets your love of music, or you'll never forget the way they looked after you that week you broke your arm.

Listen, you don't have to get all gushy and emotional, just be on the lookout for opportunities to let people know how much they matter to you, and why. Sometimes we don't realize what our best qualities are if we're not told, and if your nearest and dearest aren't going to say the words, who will?

How many people do you know who have lost someone important and wished afterwards that they'd told them, when they were alive, how much they loved them? Not that you need to wait until someone is on their deathbed. Just make it normal to let your closest friends and family know how much you appreciate, value or love them. You'll never regret it. So what's to lose?

RULE 53

Don't take anyone for granted

"Avoid unnecessary displays of emotion"

This rule follows on very nicely from the last one, and now we're getting more specific.

It's a funny thing, but scientists have found that people who literally count their blessings are happier (on average) than those who don't. Appreciating people properly is good for you and for them.

A closely related principle is that thanking people makes you feel better. We may in fact have Rule 34 to thank here,* since thanking people makes them feel good (yes, despite the fact that no one can make you feel anything, but people can choose to feel good when we thank them). And, as Rule 34 tells us, helping other people makes you feel good about yourself. So it all goes round in a positive, upward spiral.

Of course no one wants to be on the receiving end of overly gushing thanks. But – at least if you're British like me – there's a strange convention that while we're perfectly comfortable saying thank you when it's a social nicety ('Please can you pass the salt? Thanks'), we're pretty hopeless at saying thank you when we actually mean it. And that's going too far in the other direction.

So, who can you thank today? Your friends, your family, your brothers and sisters? The postman? The woman behind the shop counter, or the chap who stopped for you at the zebra crossing when it was raining? The call centre person you were on the phone to for 15 minutes who treated you like a person instead of a number? Come on, I'm sure there are lots of people you can thank.

---

* There. I feel better already.

If you really want to help these people feel good (and you do, of course), let them know precisely why you're thanking them. It's good at the end of a work phone call to be told, 'Thank you' but it's even better to be told, 'You've been very patient and I appreciate it'. The more specific you are, the more sincere you sound. So do your best to let people know why you're thanking them (apart from the chap who stopped at the zebra crossing who you didn't actually get to speak to).

Right. Are you ready to go one better? Once in a while, write a letter – oh, alright then, an email – to someone you have real reason to be grateful to. Set out clearly what it is you appreciate so much, and why it has made such a difference to you. Maybe they've given you practical help, or perhaps it's emotional support. Maybe you want to thank your parents for doing such a good job of bringing you up, or to let an old teacher know what a difference they made to your life.

Can you imagine how you would feel if you received such a letter? If so, you'll realize what you're doing for the person you're writing to. What a lovely way to repay them for their support and kindness. And I can tell you (yes, from experience) that simply sending such a letter – sorry, email – will make you feel terrific. Even before you get their reply.

RULE 54
Say thank you
out loud

"The internet makes you anonymous"

It's so easy, sitting all on your own in your bedroom or back room with your pet computer (I think of them a bit like pets), to think that no one can see you. Well, that's because no one *can* see you. You use your computer like a mask. But unlike a mask – or at least unlike the ones in *Scooby-Doo* – your computer doesn't conceal your real identity. You may feel a level of detachment from your social networking pages or your emails, but the people who read them are very conscious that those words or pictures come straight from you.

So you have to take responsibility for what you say and do online. If you wouldn't say a thing to someone's face, don't say it on Facebook either. Be considerate about what pictures you post, or the tone of the emails you send. The fact that someone reads something in privacy, on their own, doesn't make it easier for them to cope if it upsets them. It can be far worse because they don't have people around to support them, or body language to show you're not being serious.

Cyber-bullying, as it's sometimes termed in the press, isn't necessarily deliberate. It can be the result of thoughtlessness about who will see what and how they'll interpret it. Or it can result from comments being badly worded so they sound harsher than they're intended to. Run whatever you write through a mental filter before you post or send it.

I can remember reading a particularly sharply worded email once from a business associate I thought I was on good terms with. It made me feel so uncomfortable that I asked a colleague to read it for me. 'Take a look!' I said, 'Why do you think he's being so niggly today? Is it me, or do you reckon he's having a bad day?' My colleague read it through twice, and then said, 'I can't see what your problem is. It sounds perfectly friendly to me'. She then proceeded to read it aloud and, sure enough, with the inflection she put on it, it sounded fine. 'No', I replied, 'it doesn't say that. Here's what it says . . .' and I read it out my way. Exactly the same words, but a completely different interpretation. In the end it seemed sensible to assume it was intended to be friendly. But it shows how hard it is for people to interpret the tone of your posts and comments and emails, in the absence of intonation, inflection, tone of voice, facial expression and body language. A phrase such as 'Can you deal with it ASAP?' could easily be seen as either sharp or polite depending on the reader's mood, and the likely context. There's nothing else to go on.

In the old days, this was a potential problem with letters. But people thought long and hard about the letters that they wrote. A lot of the joy – but also a potential downside – of emails and the internet is that you can bang out a sentence or two really fast and send it on its way before you've thought about it.

So let's be clear. Rules are Rules. And if you wouldn't do it or say it offline, you don't do it or say it online. And if in doubt, don't.

RULE 55
The Rules don't stop online

"Always seek to improve yourself"

There's improvement, and there's flogging a dead horse. Certainly it's in your interests and everyone else's to be as good as you can at some things. Where strong positive values are concerned, of course it's a good idea to be as kind, thoughtful, trustworthy, fair, honest, helpful, selfless as you can.

But when it comes to skills, it's just silly to try to be good at everything. No one can manage that. There aren't enough hours in the day. I remember my music teacher at school telling us all that we must always try to 'improve ourselves'. And our various sports teachers. And our art teachers, and drama teachers, and all our other teachers.

The fact is that it's enormously good for your confidence to work hard at something and feel yourself getting better all the time. Realizing that you're evolving from a passable football player to a really good one, or from a decent singer to an excellent one is a great feeling. It's worth some blood, sweat and tears to achieve that.

But we're not all cut out to be brilliant footballers or angelic singers. Personally I couldn't see the point of seeking 'always to improve' in music when I was tone deaf and clearly never going to be able to sing in tune. I have a rather good singing voice actually, but only if you don't mind what notes you listen to. What would be the point in working away at something I could never excel in, when I could be putting that effort and time into something I did have a chance at? It's actually very good for us to be weak at some things. It should teach us a bit of humility, and remind us to be grateful for those strengths we do have.

So whether it's work or play, pick the things that matter to you, and that you have a chance of achieving, and work hard at those.

I've never met anyone who was brilliant at everything, and I probably wouldn't like them if I did. So let's not bother to aim for that. Let's recognize where we're never going to succeed and stop trying. Not so we can sit around and stare into space, but so we can divert that time and energy to where it can be used more profitably.

One reason we can't be good at everything is because some skills are simply not compatible with others. For example, there are two editors I often work with at my publishers. Sometimes, inevitably, there are disagreements among the team of accountants, sales people, marketing people and so on. When it comes to resolving these, one of my editors is a brilliant diplomat, and the other is terrific at making a stand for the things she believes are important, even if that means being blunt at times. These two sets of skills can both be extremely useful – but are incompatible with each other. The diplomat couldn't possibly bring herself to be so outspoken. And if my outspoken editor was enough of a diplomat to worry all the time about other people's agendas, she'd lose the ability to lay it on the line when that's what is needed. If she sought 'always to improve' her diplomatic skills she'd have to abandon her existing strength.

So accepting our shortcomings isn't an excuse to tell ourselves we're rubbish and there's no point trying. We all have strengths, and we owe it to ourselves to find out what they are and develop them. It's just about being realistic.

RULE 56
Accept your shortcomings

"Strive for perfection"

I have one writer friend who has been working on a book for the last 17 years. It's almost there – has been for about 15 of those years. But he doesn't want to publish it until it's absolutely perfect. I can understand that, but on the other hand most writers could have published at least 10 books in that time. I know some who could have produced over 100. So is my friend's perfectionism worthwhile?

I'd say no. I'd say that the way he's going, he'll be dead before he completes the book. And a book no one will ever get to read is, arguably, no book at all. It's far better to finish the thing than to keep tinkering over details which, I suspect, no one but him would notice.

The fact is that you have to factor into your definition of perfection not only the standard of work, and possibly the cost, but also whether it actually happens or not. Often there's a specific timescale that you should be within if the work is to be deemed perfect. Suppose you're writing a dissertation for your university degree. However well written it is, if you don't actually deliver it on time because you want it to be 'perfect', it has failed in its purpose. So it isn't perfect after all.

This applies at work, school and at home. Perfectionism is made out to be a positive trait. Certainly it's not good to be slapdash, and you should aim to produce work of the highest standard you can. But honestly, there's a limit. You have to balance perfection of execution against time and cost.

Do you think that when Michelangelo finished painting the ceiling of the Sistine Chapel he thought it couldn't be improved? I'll bet he didn't. I reckon he could have spent hours looking at it thinking, 'Ooh, I meant to go back over that bit of tree. And I could just tweak that nose . . . Actually, I'm wondering now about the colour of those robes . . .' However, he understood that it was as important to have the thing done as it was to perfect every tiny detail. It was good enough. I can vouch for that – I've seen it, and I thought it passed muster.

Shakespeare went back and fiddled with some of his plays for later performances. So that means he didn't think they were perfect. But he had an audience to entertain and a company of actors who needed to perform in order to eat. So his definition of perfection had to include getting the job finished on time.

You see, striving for perfection can hold you back from completing a project. And an incomplete project isn't perfect. So you're hankering after something that doesn't really exist. Of course you must do the best job you can, but that can include settling for not quite perfect.

RULE 57
Perfection can be a handicap

"You are the product of your genes"

It's certainly true that your genes play a big part in who you are. But you're no slave to them. You can change a great deal about yourself despite your genetic inheritance. You may be stuck with most of your physical characteristics (though it's amazing how much difference cosmetics can make) but you have plenty of control over your character, your outlook, your values, your attitudes, your understanding, your achievements.

You must have seen siblings who have grown up together and then taken very different paths in life. Maybe your own parents and their brothers and sisters did, or your grandparents, or close friends. One stays close to where they grew up, and the other goes off into the big wide world. After a few years, you can see that they've grown into very different people. Sometimes you can even see it when they've both stayed in their home town, but led very divergent lives.

It's what you do that counts. The older you get, the more you're formed by your experiences. Your choices will determine who you are, whether you travel, work with the disadvantaged, do drugs, choose a particular type of TV programme or computer game, spend time with your family, pursue further education, spend your weekends walking in the hills, keep dogs, live frugally, have kids, seek adventure, fight your way up the career ladder, choose a quiet life. All of these things, over the years, will become part of you and take over from your genes in deciding who you become. That's why siblings – even twins – can grow so different beyond just genetic factors.

In fact, even the things you thought were genetic can be influenced by your choices in life. As Abe Lincoln said: 'Every man over 40 is responsible for his face.'

Yep, it's down to you to become the kind of person you want to be. You can't just sit around and expect it to happen. If you want to be a go-getter you have to go and get something. If you want to do good works, find someone needy and help them. If you want to be a career high flyer, start putting focus and effort into it. Not tomorrow or next week but now, today, right here. Stop telling yourself you're going to do this or that some day. If you're serious about it, get on with it. If you're not, drop it and find something else to work towards.

If you spend your life in dark corners, you'll turn into a dark person, just like Gollum. If you want to be a sunny person, do sunny things. You're not just passing the time – you're creating yourself. So make sure you spend your time on the things that will turn you into who you want to be.

RULE 58

You are the sum of your experiences (so make them good)

"Tomorrow is another day"

You know how easy it is to fritter away an hour, or a morning, without meaning to. Well, hard as it is to believe this when you're young, it's just as easy to fritter away a whole life. Be conscious of where your time is going, because that's where your life is going.

Perhaps you spend several hours a day playing computer games. Is that why humans evolved? Or maybe you watch endless TV, involving yourself in other people's lives – possibly even fictional – rather than living your own. Or you might be waiting for that perfect job to come along, or for any job to come along. And meantime you're just metaphorically twiddling your thumbs. You know you're wasting time, but you won't carry on for ever. You'll change your ways soon.

Look, the easiest time to change bad habits is now. If you're not going to give up wasting time now, while you're acknowledging that it needs to happen, why would you give up tomorrow or next month?

If this is you, stop it. Stop it now. This will become all your life is worth, if you let it. Make every day count for something – however small – and recognize that you deserve to have a life that's worth living. Don't get sucked into pointlessness.

Of course you can watch a bit of TV, play computer games from time to time, wait for a good job (but do something while you're waiting, rather than nothing). Life is precious and frittering away even a year or two of it when you're young is more than you can spare. I don't care if you're not doing something 'worthy'. It's fine with me if you're not 'furthering your career' or 'making something of yourself' or following any other pompous edict. But I do care that you piece together a life that has some meaning.

You could make a difference to other people. You could get out and enjoy the countryside. You could develop a skill – another language, skateboarding, flower arranging. Just keep learning and growing. Maybe your job is stimulating, or you're raising a family. These things can be enough – for a while. But all those little things you do, day in and day out, from signing forms to doing the laundry, will be what make up your life. You probably can't avoid most of them from time to time, but listen to life whooshing through the gaps between the chores, and let it carry you along somewhere, rather than simply pass you by.

RULE 59

How you spend your day is how you spend your life

"There aren't enough hours in the day"

Some days you're just always in a rush and running to catch up with yourself. Maybe it seems like that's most days for you. There's always so much to do, so many meetings, phone calls, piles of laundry, emails, classes, social activities, whatever your days are generally filled with. By the time you sit down in the evening – if you even get to do that – you're exhausted. What's more, you probably feel frustrated and dissatisfied that you still have a long list of things to carry over to tomorrow.

Sound familiar? So what can you do about it? Well, actually, quite a lot. The key is to start the day with a shorter list. That way you can work steadily but without any sense of rush or stress, and get it all done. Of course there will be the odd day when the car breaks down, or a big client places a panic order, but if your workload is manageable you'll be able to catch up within a day or two when that happens.

I know what you're thinking. You're thinking it's all very well, but the list of things you *have* to do is just too long, and obviously you'd shorten it if you could, but you *just can't*. But hang on, you're going to get to the end of the day with some of those things not ticked off your list, aren't you? That's what we're talking about. I'm just saying that if they're not going to be crossed off at the end of the day, don't have them on the list at the beginning of the day. Putting them there and then not doing them isn't helping anyone. If you only have a 'to do' list that you can actually complete, you'll feel satisfied and pleased with yourself at the end of the day, instead of feeling frustrated. And meanwhile you'll have achieved exactly the same amount.

So what to leave off? Well, that's easy. You leave off all the things that you're going to push aside when the crunch comes – the ones you won't have ticked off by this evening. Come on, you know which ones those are. The only effect of having those on your list is to make you feel stressed, guilty, worried and miserable at the end of the day when you haven't done them.

Of course, there is another effect of leaving these things off your list each day. It will mean that you stop being a rushed, mildly manic person telling everyone how busy you are, and you turn into an efficient and in-control person who knows how to relax at the end of the day.

RULE 60
Know your limitations

"Always get off on the right foot from the start"

My wife used to be a stage manager in the theatre, many years ago. On one of her first jobs as a humble ASM, she arrived a few days before the opening of a new play. She quietly kept her head down, kept out of everyone's way, and did as she was told. A few days later, the set was put together and furnished for the first time. The director and designer and senior staff were deep in debate about a problem they had discovered. One side of the set looked far too empty. They couldn't put a new piece of furniture there, because the actors had been rehearsing for three weeks without it and wouldn't have time to adapt all their moves. Anyway, they couldn't afford to hire any more furniture.

At this point my wife asked if she could make a suggestion. The director and designer hadn't even learnt her name at this point, and seemed sceptical about her being able to help, but they were prepared to listen to anything as this had been holding them up now for an hour or two. My wife said, 'Do you think that if you moved the rug over to that side of the stage it would fill the visual gap without getting in the way of anything?' So they tried the idea, it worked, and everyone was very grateful. Not only that, but because it was the first time they'd noticed her, it gave her – at least for a short time – a 100 per cent record of being brilliant. So they got it into their heads that she was a smart cookie, and despite her making as many duff suggestions as everyone else after that, they never shrugged off that first impression that she was worth listening to.

She uncovered a great Rule here for any new situation in work or education. It's an excellent principle for getting off to the right start with teachers, tutors, lecturers, colleagues and managers. Impress them with the intelligence of your first comment or question and they'll mentally mark you down as a potential star student. When you start a new job, it's tempting to be so eager to get stuck in that you come out with any suggestion you can, however lame (and we all make lame suggestions sometimes). Far better to stand back and observe, and pick your moment carefully to step in with a well-judged contribution that will get you noticed instantly.

Keep quiet until you're sure you have something really worthwhile to say, and make sure the first time people notice you, it's for something that really makes you stand out in the best possible way. It might be an hour or a week before your opportunity presents itself, so just keep out of the limelight until it does. And if it really feels too long, then think up a smart question to ask, if you haven't got something specific to say. But watch and listen and be vigilant, and sooner or later your moment will come. Grasp it, make that great impression, and find yourself instantly elevated to a higher level of respect from the people who matter.

RULE 61

Bide your time to make a good impression

"Confident people know where they're going"

Oh no they don't. Some confident people *think* they know where they're going. Some people know where they're headed in one respect or another – they have a career plan, or a dream of where they'd like to live, or an idea that they'd like to settle and have kids, or that they definitely don't want kids. A few people even have some thoughts about how they're going to reach these goals. But none of us really has a clue.

I know some people look enviably confident, but it is just a veneer. Either that or they've learnt to be at ease with feeling lost, so they take it in their stride more readily. You see, no one can possibly know for sure where they're going. That's part of what makes life such fun. It's always worth having a plan – if you're going for a long hike you'd be wise to take a map, even if you're sure which paths you'll be following. A game plan is very useful, but even if you haven't got yours sorted out yet, don't imagine that puts you way behind everyone else, because it doesn't. They'll all find it much harder to adapt when life throws them bouncers, whereas you'll find it easier to go with the flow.

Sooner or later you'll work out what you want, and you'll have something to work towards. But even if you reach it, it won't necessarily be by the road you expected. I spent years trying unsuccessfully to become a writer, while doing all sorts of other jobs. Kept getting knock-backs from publishers. Then, out of the blue, a friend of mine was asked to write a book which he didn't want to do, but gave my name to his agent. It all came together from there. Those years of writing to publishers were entirely unnecessary.

For most of us it gets better as we get older. But we're still pretty lost. We just get better at looking as if we know where we're going. Sometimes it all goes swimmingly for a while, and then life lands some completely unexpected blow that throws everything off course.

It's easy to feel that you're the only one who hasn't a clue. And that makes you feel even worse, and knocks your confidence further. But I promise you, we're all pretty lost. At least if we have any sense. Because life blows you this way and that, so even if you can see your goal, you might not get there. I know a couple who were very settled and happy, careers going well, probably thought they knew where life was headed. One lunchtime they ate some mushrooms they'd foraged locally – something they'd often done before. Bang! Their life turned upside down in a few hours. Both of them were on dialysis for the next few years, unable to work properly.

So having a clear plan is useful, but it's no guarantee. Meanwhile, lots of people out there are trying to look much more confident than they feel. So don't sweat over it – you're certainly not alone.

RULE 62
Everyone else is as lost as you

"Stand out from the crowd"

The comedian Eddie Izzard used to do a great stand-up routine which included a section about shower mixer taps, and how you can turn them through 180 degrees or more, but there's only one tiny fraction of a degree where they're actually giving you water of the right temperature: 'Turn, turn, turn, turn for hot. Turn, turn, turn, turn for cold. But the only position we're interested in is the position between there . . . and there. One nanomillimetre between fantastically hot, and f****** freezing.'*

Well, exactly the same thing applies to everyone who chooses to strike a really strong image. If you want to go through life blending in with the crowd, that's fine. Lots of people are happiest that way, and it's certainly the easy option.

If you want to stand out, however, you need to recognize that you walk a very fine line. Whether it's the way you act, the way you dress, the car you drive or the company you keep, please remember that – just like Izzard's shower controls – it goes ordinary, ordinary, ordinary, ordinary, ubercool . . . total prat.

What's more, you can get so used to your own image in the mirror that you lose the ability to distinguish between the two. I'm sure you can think of examples in public life, but I'd better not mention any names. People who used to be cool and then pushed it just that bit too far, and suddenly became very embarrassing.

It's easy to get carried along with your own momentum. One minute you're looking a bit quirky, the next you're pretty eccentric, and before you know it you're right on the edge. You don't even notice how far you've come or how close you are to the edge. You

---

* It's funnier when he tells it.

feel a little heady and enjoy all the attention and adulation. And then, without realizing it . . . you tip over the other side.

I'm telling you this because somebody has to. If you choose to walk this path, you would do best to collect some very honest friends around you, and then listen to what they're telling you. I don't say you should or you shouldn't. You're welcome to look like a prat if you want to. I just think you should be warned.

RULE 63

There's a fine line between being ubercool and being a total prat

---

"Appearances matter"

Every morning when I get out of bed I look in the mirror. I think, 'I'm looking more awake than yesterday', or 'I'm sure the rings under my eyes have got darker', or occasionally, 'Yes – you don't look too bad today'. Funnily, though, I don't think these things when I look at other people. I just don't notice (unless it's quite extreme) how they compare with the last time I saw them. They just look like themselves.

And the reverse is true – they're quite oblivious to the rings under my eyes or even, sadly, the times when I really don't look too bad. That's because, as we established in Rule 41, it's not all about you. Nobody else cares or notices.

I know what you're thinking. You're thinking that's all very well if you're just looking a bit tired, but what I don't know is that you have a really huge ugly nose, or weigh 20 stone, or have terrible teeth. Actually, I don't need to know that, because the principle still holds. Everyone else is worrying about how *they* look, not about how you look.

Did you want to point out that studies have shown that attractive people have advantages in life? I know they do. And so do hard-working people, and likeable people, and determined people, and people with lots of friends, and all sorts of other people. Look, even if you're right that you're pug-ugly (which I doubt) there are still so many ways you can give yourself advantages that are within your control.

How will you find a partner if you're so repellent to look at, you want to know. Well, how did half the people you pass in the street find partners? Plenty of them don't look so special. OK, you may find it a bit harder to pick up a one-night stand if you insist on hanging out where all the beautiful people go, but I'd class that as a distinct advantage. When it comes to a long-term partner, anyone worth having will see past your looks. Actually, correction, what they'll do is focus on the beautiful aspects of you. We all have them. They won't notice your huge nose because they'll be gazing into those lovely eyes of yours (you've never noticed them, because you're too busy looking at your nose). They'll see your dazzling smile and not your weight. And most of all, they'll see the real you underneath the surface. Trust me, the worst-looking people find partners, and they find people who really love them for who they are, and so will you.

But do you know what will make the most difference of all? Your own confidence in yourself. Because confidence is really attractive, in men and women. Learn to ignore the bits of your body you aren't happy with, and focus on the bits you like best. And then flaunt them. Don't skulk around trying not to be seen, but show off that fabulous hair, or the way you can wear the latest fashions, or those beautiful hands. Once you learn to like the way you look, so will the people around you. It won't occur to them that you're not as attractive as you seem because as far as they're concerned – that's right – it's not all about you.

RULE 64
Be happy with the way you look

"It's just a drop in the ocean"

Gandhi said, 'Whatever you do in life will be insignificant, but it is very important that you do it'. Philosophers can argue back and forth exactly what he meant, and he probably meant many things. One of those is that small actions can seem insignificant but they are what make up the big stuff. We saw this in Rule 59 about how you spend your day, but it counts in other ways too.

Essentially, you have to do what you believe in, even if you don't believe it will make a difference. Suppose you think it's really important to boycott companies that use child labour. Then you see some stunning product from one of those companies that you really want. It's easy to tell yourself that this company has millions of customers, and just one purchase from you will make no difference in the grand scheme of things. Well, you may be right that it's insignificant, but it's still very important that you stick to your principles. The only thing that will persuade these companies to change their practices will be millions of insignificant boycotts like yours. If each person counts themselves out on the grounds of how minuscule their own influence is, the change will never happen.

Each action or decision is tiny in itself, but that's how you build up the whole. Just as a butterfly flapping its wings in China can change the weather in New York,* so each whole can only be the sum of its parts. That's how democracy works. You may feel that your one vote will count for nothing, but millions of people just like you, all casting their insignificant votes, can bring governments down.

---

* According to Chaos Theory. I'm not going into all that now.

Sometimes you're convinced that it really won't make any difference to the whole. You just know that everyone else *isn't* going to vote the same way as you, or just won't go to the trouble of a boycott. And you may be right. But it's still important to do what you believe should be done.

You may think that it doesn't matter what you do because nobody is watching. This tiny, teensy insignificant thing will go entirely unnoticed, and no one will be any the wiser. But you'd be wrong. Someone *is* watching: you are. You also have to carry out these insignificant acts because it's the only way to be true to yourself. You are defined by your choices and if you betray your own beliefs, you change yourself. If a thing is right, it's right. So however insignificant the results of your choice, it's still important that you make it.

RULE 65
The insignificant is important

"The job comes first"

If you come from the kind of background where most people have serious careers – and very possibly even if you don't – there can be a load of pressure to get yourself stuck into a career that has 'good prospects' and a potentially high salary. Parents, teachers, friends, all of them can push you in this direction. And when you start on the first rungs of that ladder, your colleagues and managers will step the pressure up even more.

You'll start to do well, and get regular promotions and pay rises. Of course you'll have to put in long hours, and maybe work some weekends. There might be quite a bit of travelling too. The boss will call you in the evening or on a Sunday – but that's OK because it makes you feel important and needed. Holidays may be hard to arrange, but you can probably manage a few days if you take your smartphone and laptop and get some work done while you're away.

Let me be clear: I'm not saying that jobs like this are a bad thing. For many people they're wonderful. They're stimulating and exciting and they keep you on your toes. There are bad days, but often the stress is very positive and buzzy. Don't let me put you off this kind of career, whether it's in teaching, business, politics, media or scientific research. Or anything else.

However . . . there is more to life than your career. There are people: friends, family, partner, kids. It's people who really make life worthwhile. And if you really sink yourself into a high-pressure career for too long, you'll find that all of those people drift away, or never come to pass. And one day – when you retire, or get made redundant – you'll wonder what you have left, and what it was all for.

Big exciting careers are great, and for the first few years after leaving school or uni it's fine to bury yourself in your work, but by the time you reach your mid to late twenties you need to be aware that there's more to life. Don't let it all slip by. Don't end up with no partner, or partners who keep leaving you, because you can't give your attention to anything outside your job.

Even if you don't want a relationship or kids, you still need an escape from what you do most of the time. You need friends who can take you away from all that for a while. These friends aren't going to appear out of the ether. You have to go out and find them, and then give them enough attention so that they stick around. They'll understand that your job keeps you busy a lot of the time, so long as you make sure there's some time for them too.

Don't keep promising yourself you'll free up more time in a year or two, or after the next promotion. Set a firm date and stick to it. You don't have to give up the job – just make sure it allows you a proper life too.

RULE 66
Don't mistake your career for your life

"Get it all out in the open"

It's not clever you know, having a go at someone. Not just because it isn't nice, but because whatever it is you want, it sets your cause back considerably. Which isn't smart.

Some people just thrive on conflict. Any excuse and they're flinging insults and pushing people to give in to them. I know it isn't always easy, especially if it's what you've grown up with, but there are other ways to handle tricky situations. If you look for conflict you can always find it. But if you seek to avoid it, it's almost never necessary.

The whole thing with conflict – pretty much what defines it – is that you set yourself up in opposition to the other person. It becomes a battle where one person will ultimately win (you, you hope) and the other will lose. But of course no one wants to be the one who loses, so whoever is on the side that's losing will keep battling rather than admit defeat. And so it goes on.

Far better to address the problem in a way that doesn't have two sides to start with. Present yourself as being on the same side as the other person, both jointly trying to deal with the issue, whatever it is.

So when you see a problem looming in which you need someone else to change their position, don't set up a conflict in the first place. Find a way to deal with it assertively, but not aggressively, so that together you can find a way through. It can come down to no more than the choice of words you use.

Suppose someone in your house keeps loading the dishwasher badly and half the dishes are still dirty at the end of the wash. Very irritating. You could say, 'You keep putting the dishes in the wrong places and too close together and it's really annoying me'. Or you could say, 'Half of the pots in the dishwasher are still dirty again. I wonder what we can do about it?' Now imagine being on the receiving end of those two alternatives. The first would probably make you defensive, and quite possibly start a row. The second would make you think that perhaps there is a better way to do something. See? Much smarter.

Sometimes other people come at you with a challenging remark almost guaranteed – maybe even designed – to provoke conflict: 'We should throw out the dishwasher and go back to washing up by hand. Then you couldn't keep telling me I've stacked it wrong.' The smartest response here, rather than rise to the argument, is simply not to react at all. If they actually start wrangling the dishwasher out of the house you can intervene, but almost certainly the comment wasn't serious and was only intended to create conflict. They won't really follow it through.

Now just one thing. Don't go too far the other way, will you? If you're scared of conflict you'll sidestep issues which need to be addressed, and that's not good. I'm not asking you to avoid difficult situations. Just to find another way of dealing with them.

RULE 67
Avoid conflict

"If you know you're in the right, don't back down"

As with several of these Rules to break, there are times when this Rule holds. It's a matter of not applying it blindly. So if you know you're in the right over an important ethical matter of principle and values, you should indeed not back down. Suppose someone is treating another person badly and you decide to intervene – in that instance you should hold your ground. Even so, that's better done by being calm, rational and civil. And when I say 'better done', I mean 'more likely to work'.

On all other occasions, however, the fact that you're right is less important than reaching an agreement. You may well be right that this fence belongs to you, or that you are technically senior, or that precedent is in your favour. Then again, very often the person you're in a disagreement with is equally sure that they are in the right. Maybe they are. Maybe you both are. It doesn't matter.

What matters is that you reach an agreement, and that entails compromise. The idea of compromise is often seen as some kind of giving in, which implies losing face. However, that's not actually what it means at all. It means that you both adapt in order to resolve things. That sounds reasonable, doesn't it?

Focus on the fact that you want a solution to the dispute. In fact, take encouragement from the fact that you both want a solution. You both have more to gain by resolving things than you do by leaving them as they are. So if you can engineer that, you haven't lost face at all. You've succeeded.

You'll need to be civil, for a start. No one will do a deal with you if you're ranting at them. If they're the one ranting, you'll need to stay calm and civil to have any chance of getting them to calm down.

Next, you have to look at the situation from their perspective. Why is it so important to them? Why do they think they're the one who is right? Do they have a point? And having thought that through, rationally and fairly, you can think about what they really need out of an agreement for it to work. Suppose your neighbour is arguing with you about whether you can park in front of their house. Are they simply being territorial (which is a natural human instinct, even if they have no legal case), or are they concerned about where they will park, or whether their wheelie bins will be blocked?

Once you can see where the other person is coming from – without having to agree with it – you should be able to suggest a solution that will keep everyone happy. And when you arrive at that compromise, and both adapt to each other, you can pat yourself on the back. Achieving compromise is more demanding than just arguing or ranting, and it's something you can be proud of.

RULE 68
Don't be afraid of compromise

"Some people are just asking for it"

I've said it before* and I'll say it again. There are many times when it's OK to state what your feelings are, but not OK to enact them. I know this is simple to say and really difficult to live up to. I do appreciate that it's tough, but you can do it. It takes a simple shift of vision, from being the sort of person who acts in a certain way, to being a different sort of person who acts in a different sort of way. Look, no matter how rough it gets you are never going to:

- take revenge

- act badly

- be very, very angry

- hurt anyone

- act rashly

- be aggressive.

That's it, the bottom line. You are going to maintain the moral high ground at all times. You are going to behave honestly, decently, kindly, forgivingly, nicely (whatever that means) no matter what the provocation. No matter what the challenge thrown at you. No matter how unfairly another behaves. No matter how badly they behave. You will not retaliate. You will carry on being good and civilized and morally irreproachable. Your manners will be impeccable, your language moderate and dignified. There is nothing they can say or do that will make you deviate from this line.

Yes, I know it's difficult at times. I know when the rest of the world is behaving appallingly and you have to carry on taking it

---

* In *The Rules of Life*. And I don't apologize for repeating it here.

on the chin without giving in to your desire to floor them with a savage word, it's really, really tough. When people are being horrid to you it's natural to want to get your own back and lash out. Don't. Once this rough time has passed you'll be so proud of yourself for keeping the moral high ground that it will taste a thousand times sweeter than revenge ever would.

I know revenge is tempting, but you won't go there. Not now, not ever. Why? Because if you do you'll be sinking to their level, you'll be at one with the beasts instead of the angels (see Rule 71), because it demeans you and cheapens you, because you will regret it, and lastly because if you do, then you're no Rules player. Revenge is for losers. Taking and keeping the moral high ground is the only way to be. It doesn't mean you're a pushover or a wimp. It just means that any action you do take will be honest and dignified and clean.

RULE 69

Keep the moral high ground

"It's good to let your feelings out"

A few decades ago you never expressed how you felt. Stiff upper lip and all that. Bottle it up, keep it in, don't burden others with it. Well, that all seems to have gone by the wayside, and by and large I've been happy to wave it a cheery goodbye. It's certainly healthier to express your feelings than to deny them.

However, just because it's good for you to say how you feel, that doesn't mean it's good to let your emotions out at any time and in any company. There's a world of difference between having a cry on your best friend's shoulder – or your mum's or your partner's – and sobbing in public or in front of whoever happens to be there at the time.

I have a friend who is an undertaker. He tells me that the most useful warning he can give his clients, when he organizes funerals for the partners or parents, or even children they've just lost, is this: 'Be prepared to spend the whole afternoon comforting people who are less upset than you.'

How did we get from the stiff upper lip, all the way to sobbing inconsolably all over the very person who has just been bereaved – the one who has much more right to be publicly upset than you? That's the other extreme, and it's way too far. There's a selfishness to it that's almost embarrassing. It's fine to be upset at a funeral – you're there because you care – but if you can't control it you need to keep away from the immediate family.

There's a modern trend for displaying our emotions freely, as if it makes us a better person. But sometimes* it's not all about you. Sometimes other people's emotions are more important than your

---

* Here comes Rule 41 again . . .

own, and you need to keep yours in abeyance for a while. You can go home later and sob all over the cat, or phone your best friend for some comfort. While you're with people who have more cause than you to feel frightened, grief-stricken, upset, anxious, miserable, allow them the space for it without adding to their problems.

This isn't only about times of deep grief or trauma. It's all too commonplace, when someone says, 'I've had a dreadful day', to respond, 'Tell me about it! My day was a real shocker. First of all . . .' It's presented as empathy, showing that you've been there too, but in reality it's all about taking the focus of attention off the other person and putting it firmly on yourself. As if it's suddenly a competition to see who's had the worst day, who can justify the biggest outpouring of emotion.

If someone needs a moan, just listen and sympathize. Don't compete. I sometimes think we should introduce a new bit of etiquette that says only one person at a time is allowed to have a moan — and it's first come, first served.

RULE 70

Don't trample on other people's emotions

"No one is perfect"

This fake Rule is too often just an excuse for making bad choices. Of course we don't always get it right, we're not always perfect, but if we follow that as a principle it just becomes a get-out clause.

Listen, every single day of our lives we are faced with an immense number of choices. And each and every one of them usually boils down to a simple choice between being on the side of the angels or the beasts.* Which are you going to pick? Or did you not even realize what was going on? Let me explain. Every action we take has an effect on our family, people around us, society, the world in general. And that effect can be positive or negative – it's usually our choice. And sometimes it is a difficult choice. We get torn between what *we* want and what is good for others: personal satisfaction or magnanimity.

Look, no one said this was going to be easy. And making the decision to be on the side of the angels is often a tough call. But if we want to succeed in this life – in terms of how close we get to generating self-satisfaction, happiness, contentment – then we consciously have to do this. This can be what we dedicate our lives to – angels and not beasts.

If you want to know if you have already made the choice, just do a quick check of how you feel and how you react if someone cuts in front of you in a line of traffic in the rush hour. Or when you're in a big hurry and someone stops you to ask for directions. Or if your brother or best friend gets in trouble with the police. Or when you lend money to a friend and they don't pay it back. Or if your boss calls you a fool in front of the rest of your colleagues. Or your neighbour's trees start to encroach on your property. Or you hit your thumb with a hammer. Or, or, or. As I

---

* I've written this before, in *The Rules of Life,* and it's worth repeating in case you haven't seen it before. Or have seen it but could do with a reminder.

said, it is a choice we have to make every day, lots of times. And it has to become a conscious choice to be effective.

Now, the problem is that no one is going to tell you exactly what constitutes an angel or a beast. Here you are going to have to set your own parameters. But come on, it can't be that difficult. I think an awful lot of it is self-evident. Does it hurt or hinder? Are you part of the problem or the solution? Will things get better or worse if you take certain actions? You have to make this choice for yourself alone.

It is your interpretation of what is an angel or beast that counts. There is no point telling anyone else they are on the side of the beasts, as they may have a totally different definition. What other people do is their choice and they won't thank you for telling them otherwise. You can of course watch as an impassive, objective observer and think to yourself: 'I wouldn't have done it like that', or 'I think they just chose to be an angel', or even, 'Gosh, how beastly'. But you don't have to say anything.

RULE 71

Be on the side of the angels, not the beasts

"Meet your deadlines"

This is a very practical Rule, but an important one. I was brought up to understand that I shouldn't let people down, and I should always do things when I say I will. And quite right too, as I'm sure you'll agree. 'Meet your deadlines', I was told.

Ah, but I can't begin to tell you how many times I got into trouble trying to meet deadlines. From school assignments right through to publishers' manuscript deadlines, I've gone through hell in those last few hours or days trying to get things done. There are so many last-minute problems that get in the way.

If you've had a few months to write a book, it just sounds ridiculous to say to your publisher on delivery day, 'I'm really sorry I haven't quite finished the book. You see, my mum was taken really ill a couple of days ago . . .' They'll just wonder what you were up to for the last few months.

The same goes for reports or presentations at work, dissertations at uni, buying birthday presents, clearing out of the flat you're leaving, and anything else you can think of. All of them are deadlines that you can plan for perfectly, and then something can come along and scupper those plans. And it will scupper them when there's no leeway left, no slack. So you have no option but to miss the deadline, or abandon your ailing mother or whatever it was that got in the way.

Listen, I can guarantee you that stuff will *always* get in the way of your deadlines. I don't even need to know what you're supposed to be doing and when it has to be completed. I already know that spanners will fling themselves into the works. They always do. The car breaks down, the computer crashes, the trains stop running, your best friend has a crisis, someone is ill, you run out of materials (after the shops have shut, needless to say), you get interrupted, someone senior demands your presence at a vital meeting, the deadline gets brought forward, the weather gets in the way.

You may not know what will disrupt your schedule at the last minute, but be aware that something absolutely will. And if you're not expecting it, not only will you miss the deadline, but you'll become hugely stressed and irritable and frustrated. The one thing you won't want to accept is that it's your own fault. I know this because I've been there time and again, and it's never my fault.

Except that deep down I know it is. And after years of trouble, I now know how to prevent it happening except on the very rarest of occasions. I've stopped trying to meet deadlines, and I now aim to stay ahead of them. I plan to complete small projects a day or two ahead of time, and big ones up to a month or two ahead. I build some slack into my timetable. I've no idea what it's waiting for, but I know that something will come along and fill it.

RULE 72
Keep ahead of deadlines

"Give good advice"

Some people find this Rule easy to break, but most struggle with it. The fact is that it's not good to give people advice if you can possibly help it. Tricky, I know, but important.

Just to clarify, it's OK to advise friends on whether this top goes with these trousers, or what wine to drink with the meal, or where to get their car tyres replaced. I'm talking about emotional stuff here – whether to leave their girlfriend, how to handle their difficult mother, whether to quit their job. These are often big decisions too, which makes it even more important that you don't tell them what to do.

The fact is that these things are based heavily on feelings. Your friend's feelings, not yours. Only they know how they really feel, how they will feel in a particular scenario, what they will or won't regret, what the nuances of a situation or a relationship are. These are bespoke decisions, that can't be fixed with off-the-peg solutions.

Besides, what if you're wrong? What if they follow your advice and it all goes horribly wrong? What will that do to your friendship? Or suppose they ignore your advice and it all goes wrong? Or they ignore you and it turns out great – what does that say about you? Or (and this is not uncommon) you advise them to leave their partner, probably explaining why you don't like them or trust them, and they end up staying together. And now your friend knows that you don't like/trust their partner. Another fine mess you've got yourself into.

So just keep your mouth shut. You don't know best. Leave your friends alone to make their own decisions. But that doesn't mean you can't support them. You can give them facts and figures, such as industry figures on the buoyancy of the jobs market if they're considering giving notice. And you can certainly ask them questions, but do it with balance: 'How do you think you'll feel two years from now if you leave your partner?' And then, 'How do you think you'll feel two years from now if you stay?'

You can also help by drawing your friend's attention to options they might not have considered. If they're deciding whether or not to hand in their notice at work, you can ask if they've considered waiting to see if they get promotion in the next couple of months, or asking their boss about other openings in the company, or going freelance, or handing in their notice without waiting to find another job first. Just don't tell them which option you think they should take. Your opinion is irrelevant because it's not about you.* Only they can know what will work, because only they know how they feel.

RULE 73
Don't give advice

---

* Ooh, that Rule 41 sneaks up on you every time.

"Let people know when you're right"

Suppose you warn your brother that if he doesn't get his car fixed it will break down. He doesn't do it and, sure enough, it breaks down late at night in the middle of nowhere. Or maybe you advised your friend to leave their job and they didn't listen. Now the firm is going into receivership. Or perhaps your colleague didn't believe you when you said that the company was relocating – and they've just found out you were right. Now, how are you going to respond to all these things, when it turns out you were right all along?

If you're thinking the answer is to say, 'Told you so' then go to the back of the class and stay in after lessons. You can write out 100 times 'I must not say "I told you so"'. But, of course, you're a Rules player, so you won't have been thinking any such thing, will you?

If you're following the last Rule, and not giving anyone advice, this Rule is much easier to stick to. You may privately have foreseen the outcome, but if you resisted proffering advice, well done, and now there's no temptation to say 'I told you so'.

So what's wrong with saying it? Well, the only time the phrase is ever used is when something bad has happened to someone and you predicted it. Or when something good has happened that you predicted and they failed to. So what the expression actually means is, 'Look! I'm right and you're wrong. See?'

Now just explain to me how this is ever a helpful, supportive, kind or considerate thing to say. The fact it's true is neither here nor there. The fact is you're talking to someone who is at best wrong, and at worst also in a hole because of it, and choosing to rub their nose in that fact. Is that Rules behaviour? No, it isn't.

When was the last time someone said 'Told you so' to you, and you felt grateful to them, appreciative that they'd drawn your attention to how wrong you'd been in contrast to their own rightness? When did hearing those words cause a warm feeling of love and thankfulness to flow through your veins?

Never, is my guess. Because no one wants to hear it. And I don't blame them. So next time you're right and someone else is wrong, just button it. *You* know you were right, and that will have to be enough.

RULE 74

Never say 'I told you so'

"Stick to what you're good at"

I've read a lot lately about how you should push children to do things that are challenging in order to give them more 'grit'. You know, send them on long hikes, boot camps and so on. Give them positions of responsibility and leadership to see how they handle them. And if they fail – well, apparently that develops grit just as well as succeeding at these challenges.

Hmmm. Yes and no. I think what people mean by 'grit' is a combination of self-confidence and resilience. And that's certainly a good thing to have, at any age. But, whether you're at school, uni or much further along the road, the way to achieve it is not quite so clear-cut.

I've seen kids stretched by these kinds of demanding activities who have indeed surprised themselves and derived huge confidence from succeeding. And I've seen kids come close and grow stronger despite, or because of, the fact they've ultimately failed. But I've also seen children – and adults – who have been pushed too far and have lost confidence when they haven't managed to do what they set out to do, or what other people around them have managed.

The secret is in just how far you're challenged. If you only do what you know, and never take on anything that daunts you, it's hard for you to build up your confidence and your resilience. We've already seen that mistakes and failures aren't always bad, and sometimes you impress yourself despite not ultimately succeeding. So it's really important that you say yes to things you're tempted to turn down because you're not sure you can do them.

On the other hand, a challenge that is really too far for you – whether that's organizationally, emotionally, physically, psychologically or anything else – can batter your confidence and leave you feeling vulnerable and fragile.

Only you know where the line is between a demanding but ultimately satisfying challenge, and one that will knock the stuffing out of you. But one thing I can promise you: if you never accept any challenges you're going to struggle to grow in confidence. You'll learn nothing new about yourself and you'll stagnate.

So look for challenges, whether it's organizing a wedding, going trekking in the Himalayas, taking the lead at a big corporate presentation, learning a new language, installing your kitchen yourself, or volunteering at the local soup kitchen. Keep stretching yourself, but don't feel you have to push yourself beyond your natural limits. If in doubt you can set yourself mini-challenges: run a half-marathon before you enter your name for a full marathon, or install most of the kitchen but leave the plumbing and electrics to experts.

RULE 75
Stretch yourself

"You've a right to be treated fairly"

From early childhood, we start moaning that 'it isn't fair!' And many people go on moaning in the same vein for the rest of their lives. It's surprising really, because no one ever gives us the least reason to expect life to be fair, but still we complain when it isn't.

Well, enough. Life's unfair: get over it. It starts the day you're born: into the affluent West or drought-torn sub-Saharan Africa, to decent parents or dreadful ones, with siblings or not, into wealth or poverty. Yep, it's tough, at least for some people. However unfair your life is, I'll bet I can find someone whose life is worse, through no fault of their own.

I won't give you endless stories about people who've suffered a series of truly terrible misfortunes, although I could. Chances are that you won't be in one of those real worst-case scenarios and you'll probably be lamenting over something far more trivial. Next time you miss out on the flat you wanted to rent, or have to work at the weekend, or even lose your job, or struggle to start a family, don't compare yourself with other people who have flats and jobs and families and free weekends. Try comparing yourself with the ones who have no home, no work, no money, no family.

If that's too big a stretch for your brain, then imagine that you're in a job where you're working hard, doing really well and showing your true potential. You realize there's an opportunity for your company to create a new role which would be great for the business and perfect for you. The big boss agrees, creates the new job . . . and gives it to somebody else. This isn't just a random example – it happened to two people I know in different companies at different times. Was it fair? Hell no. But is it life? Yes, of course it is. Neither of these two people whined or took it to a tribunal or claimed discrimination or whatever. They're both

Rules players and they took it on the chin and moved on to a better place.

I can tell you now that life won't treat you fairly. It may of course treat you far better than you could hope – it can be unfair in both directions. We don't appreciate the good things which means we think life is being harder on us than it really is.

So aim to notice all the good stuff that happens to you in life. Every day you're healthy, every person around you who brings you happiness, the fact you have a roof over your head and food to eat, and all the other things that some people, quite unfairly, can't count on. Life is good to most of us as often as it's bad, and we simply don't appreciate it enough. So be grateful for everything you have that not everyone else has, and then you may feel you've got a better deal than you realized. And if it's sometimes unfair to you despite all that – well, the dice have to fall somewhere, and maybe you just saved someone else. Instead of thinking, 'Why me?' try thinking, 'Why not me?'

RULE 76

Stop expecting life to be fair

"The more you learn about a subject, the more of an expert you become"

When one of my sons was 3, his ambition in life was to know everything there was to know. At that stage it seemed, to his mind, perfectly achievable. Indeed, there's a famous bumper sticker that says 'Employ a teenager, while they still know everything'.

I suppose it could be depressing to discover that when you really start to get deeply into a subject that fascinates you, the expanse of knowledge opens up and the further you get into it, the further the horizon extends. The more you learn, the more conscious you are of your own ignorance.

Of course the better way to view this is to be excited at how much there always is to learn, and to enjoy the process. What would actually be depressing would be knowing everything there is to know and being unable to enjoy the subject any more. Yes, it's daunting to find how much more there is to learn, but it gives you so much scope to get stuck into something that fascinates you. And remember, everyone else is in the same position. Even the world expert on a subject will know only the tip of the iceberg. They will, however, probably be fairly knowledgeable about the size of the iceberg – they'll understand their own areas of ignorance better than most.

What's more, the experts will also recognize that not everything accepted as fact is necessarily so, certain as it seems. The younger you are, the more often things can seem to be black and white. As you get older, most subjects appear in greyscale, with more nuances and subtleties than you realized before. This is especially true of topics such as religion and politics, not to mention more everyday – but still important – practical skills such as management or parenting.

When I was a child, I knew almost everything there was to know about dinosaurs. No one knew a lot at the time, so we were all experts. There were probably only about half a dozen dinosaurs that were widely known, and little did we realize at the time that even one of those never existed.* The real experts, however, understood how much more there was to learn. That's when you can start to call yourself an expert – when you can grasp the extent of your ignorance.

I have a friend who recently started to retrain as a psychotherapist in her forties. She researched it a fair bit before she started the training, but once she was properly underway she discovered that there were far more branches of the subject and far more training options than she'd realized. The further she got into it, the more possibilities opened up. This is the way of things, and it is both scary and thrilling. Be thrilled by it and enjoy the journey. You'll never be able to see the whole of the ocean, but you will see far more of it if you row out to the middle than you ever will if you stand on the shore just dabbling your toes.

RULE 77

The more you know, the more you don't

---

* Brontosaurus, if you're interested. It turned out to be a case of mistaken identity. However, apparently they're about to reinstate it after all, which proves the point that even experts don't know everything.

"You can't learn anything from a fool"

Think about this for a minute. Everyone really smart and successful must have been taught or managed at some point by someone less capable than themselves. Were all Einstein's teachers cleverer than him? I doubt it.

Your boss may not be as smart as you, but hopefully they are good at managing people or asking the right questions to stretch your brain – and there's a lot to be said for that. Better that than a smart boss with an attitude problem.

And a less than superbright boss or teacher doesn't have to hold you back. You just have to find new ways to learn from them.

So watch them, assess them, evaluate them. Work out where they're going wrong, as well as where they're getting it right (when they do) and think about how you would avoid making that same mistake yourself.

Thinking this deeply about it can only help reinforce the lessons for you, so really they're doing you a favour by making you think harder and more clearly.

There's a UK corporate film company that was set up in the 1970s based entirely on teaching people through others' mistakes. The company was hugely successful because it amusingly showed the wrong way to handle a situation (in sales, management or whatever). By seeing what mistakes to avoid, the tens of thousands of trainees who watched these films learnt how to get it right.

So you can do the same thing. See a weak boss or an ineffectual teacher as a learning opportunity. Work out a better way to explain the concept your teacher has just stumbled through, or plan out how you would have gone about managing that project.

These are the lessons that will really stick, so be enthusiastic about being able to learn in this way.

Every day we learn from other people's mistakes, big and small, whether they are trying to teach us or not. Life is packed with opportunities, and all you need to do is analyze where other people have gone wrong to be able to learn from them rather than getting incredibly frustrated. And it's a good thing too. After all, mistakes are a valuable learning tool, but there's no need for you to make all of them yourself.

RULE 78
Learn from other people's mistakes

"If you're going to do something, do it properly"

Like many of these Rules to Break, there are times when the Rule applies. The danger is in following it blindly. Yes, it's true that there comes a point in any project or challenge when you have to either get out or just go for it. But don't imagine that that point necessarily comes near the beginning.

Of course there are some things that you have to go for. If you decide to have children, for example, you really have to commit yourself before you actually begin. But there are many times in life when it just isn't necessary to do that. Often you can dip a toe in, and then another, and really take your time before you jump.

I grew up with a friend who hated being in the City. He really wanted to live in a particular part of the country where he'd spent his childhood holidays. The trouble was, it was several hours from London* and he didn't know a soul there. He wanted to make a clean break, leave London and set up a new life in this place. But he was very scared. It took another friend of his to convince him that he could get a job a couple of hours out of London in that direction, still live in the country, and see how he liked it. That way he could either move right on down to his dream location when he felt ready, or head back to London if he decided it was all a horrible mistake.

That's just what he did, and he stayed in the halfway house for a few years before he felt the time was right to move on. He eventually arrived where he'd always wanted to be, and is still very

---

* If you're American or Australian, I should explain that we English think that's a very long way.

happy there. In fact, he's happier than he would have been if he'd gone straight there because he made a few mistakes in the first, halfway move, which he avoided this time around. He discovered, for example, that he didn't like village life and preferred to live somewhere more remote – a useful discovery that smoothed the way for his later move.

Don't let anyone tell you that you have to go all out for big changes. Whether it's a house in a new location, a new job, a relationship commitment or anything else, if there's a way to do it in stages, that's fine. It doesn't matter what anyone else thinks. You just go at the pace that works for you. Keep moving – don't wuss out – but so long as you're making progress it's no one's business but yours what speed you move at.

RULE 79
You don't have to jump in the deep end

"Stick with what you know"

Right. I hope that last Rule reassured you and you're now feeling secure and brimming with confidence. You're going to need it. Because I now want you to step away from the familiar and try something new.

This is related to Rule 75* but it's not the same. That was about pushing yourself further than you think you can go, but it could be in a direction you're used to. This time I don't care if you don't push yourself hard, but I care about where you're going. I want you to break new ground, do something different, wake yourself up a bit. It doesn't have to be difficult, it just needs to stimulate some part of you that usually languishes in the shadows.

Go to see an opera. Say yes to an invitation you'd normally turn down without thinking. Go somewhere different on holiday. Take a dance class. Go for a walk at midnight. Dye your hair pink. Try eating calves' brains. It doesn't matter what you do, so much as that you're doing something new. What's the point in getting three score years and ten on this earth, if you're just going to keep repeating yourself?

The more you put yourself in new situations, the more you'll learn and the more you'll open your mind to other new experiences. It will give you something to think about, talk about, measure other activities against. Love it or hate it, every new experience broadens your mind. You'll meet new people and discover new sensations. And although you may hate some things, so what? You don't have to do them again. Meanwhile, along the way you'll discover some things that you love that you'd never have found without your new approach to life.

---

* Which was 'Stretch yourself'. Come on, keep up.

Every so often, an opportunity comes along that is exciting but also daunting. Maybe a job offer that sounds fantastic but means working abroad. If you've never stepped out of your same old rut it's going to be hard to say yes to it. But if you're in the habit of trying new things, embracing change – even on a small scale – you'll be able to grab the opportunity and relish it. You'll know that you can handle new experiences so you won't need to be anxious. Well, maybe just a tiny bit, because that can make it more fun.

Sir Thomas Beecham supposedly said, 'You should try everything once, except incest and Morris dancing'. I might add a few things to the list, but the gist is bang-on. It's not about the thing you're trying. It's about the fact that you're trying it.

RULE 80
Step out of your comfort zone

"People will judge you by what you own"

Ah yes, a big house, fast car, good clothes, beautiful furniture. That's how people will know that you've made a success of life. Or at least that's how shallow people will know. They'll judge success in crude, objective terms (see Rule 1) and moreover they'll measure your worth as a person by your so-called success too.

Do we care what they think? No. We do not. Anyone whose opinion is so easily won or lost, and based on such silly measures, is not worth concerning ourselves with. We will of course treat them well, but privately we won't give a fig for their opinion. Usually, it's merely a reflection of their own view of themselves. They think they've succeeded when they have the house, the car, the clothes, the furniture, so they're judging you on their terms. It says a lot about them, but nothing about you.

Look, I'm the last person to criticize anyone for a predilection for cars (although I prefer them classic rather than fast). If you have a strong aesthetic eye, by all means put things in your house that you consider beautiful and therefore make you smile. But don't acquire things for the sake of it, or because you want to impress people. It isn't necessary. Plenty of people have managed to impress without being wealthy. Mother Teresa had nothing. Gandhi wasn't generally considered flashy. It didn't stop people admiring and respecting them.

Once you start trying to live up to your perception of other people's standards, you find yourself accumulating possessions for no good purpose. William Morris said, 'Have nothing in your house that you do not know to be useful or believe to be beautiful'. You won't find a better maxim to live by. The world can do without people who accumulate things they don't want or need in order to impress others. We're using up our resources fast enough on things we actually do need.

Part of this, as you know, is about relinquishing our inner need to earn other people's approval. For some of us that can be a hard thing to do. If you don't acknowledge what's going on, it's impossible. And what's more, you'll never have enough to feel you've succeeded. Once you accept that you're collecting stuff you don't want because of what other people might think (and in fact might well not think), it's easier to train yourself to stop.

Mother Teresa and Gandhi are living proof that you don't really need all that stuff to earn respect and approval. However, it can help to find an example nearer to home too. I'll bet you have an uncle or teacher or neighbour or friend who is widely respected and who doesn't acquire stuff to impress people with. Think of them, and trust yourself to impress people by who you are, and not by what you have.

RULE 81

Don't try to keep up with the Joneses

"Hide your mistakes"

One of my brothers had an argument with a friend at college over how a certain word was spelt. The argument was amicable but quite forceful, as both of them were certain they were right, and neither was prepared to let it drop. Eventually the friend said, 'Right. I'm going to look it up in the dictionary', and off he went to his room. When he hadn't reappeared after five minutes, my brother went to track him down. He opened the door of the friend's room to find him kneeling on the floor over the dictionary, with a bottle of correction fluid in his hand, looking extremely sheepish and embarrassed at being caught.*

It was clear all along that one of them was going to be wrong, even though both of them were convinced it was the other one. The fact is that none of us is right every single time. And, you know, it just could be you who's wrong. Sometimes.

I'm not suggesting that you constantly doubt yourself, but when you find yourself in this situation, just consider that it might be you. It's fine – even the cleverest, most knowledgeable, most experienced, best informed people are wrong occasionally. So it's OK for you to be wrong too. It doesn't make you stupid, or even ignorant.

On the other hand, insisting you're right when you aren't will make you look arrogant and pig-headed. And quite possibly, like my brother's friend, very foolish. So whether you're arguing about religion or politics, whose fault something is, who owns what, or how a word is spelt, just bear in mind that it will be fine if you turn out to be wrong, but only if you've approached the subject with an open mind. Don't back yourself into a corner where being wrong will make you look foolish.

---

* This same friend coined one of my favourite phrases when – on a similar occasion when he ultimately turned out to be correct – he said, 'It's nice to be right when you're sure'.

It's not just about you and how you come across. It's also about the other person and how you treat them. There's no excuse for being boorish or overbearing or dominating or shouting someone down or not listening to their side. These are all the things you're likely to do if you go into the discussion convinced that you're right and they are stupid if they can't see it. Even if you are right, that's no excuse for this kind of behaviour.

So even if you do turn out to have been correct – this time – don't make the other person feel small and do, at all times, remember Rule 74. You've forgotten Rule 74? Go and take a look and then come back here.

There. Well done. And when it comes to Rule 74, I promise you I'm right.

RULE 82

Remember, you could be wrong – someone has to be

"Live in the present"

Well, clearly in literal terms the present is the only time you can live in. But it's taken to mean focusing on what's happening now and disregarding the past or the future. Sure, you'll have more fun if you appreciate and enjoy what you have at the time. Living in the present can stop you from feeling anxious or worrying about things you can't change.

But what if the present isn't much fun? Suppose you're already anxious or upset or grief-stricken or miserable or depressed. In that case living entirely in the present doesn't seem so clever. Of course you need to have an eye on the present in order to resolve things. But where's the sense in immersing yourself in your misery? When that happens it's much better to do a spot of living in the future or the past.

There's too much nonsense talked generally about the benefits of living in the present. Some people try to impress it on you as a permanent state. It's certainly true that when things are going well it can feel better still if you just go with the flow and enjoy yourself. But real life has a past and a future too, and they shouldn't be ignored. Sometimes enjoying 'the now'* is a good thing. But sometimes ignoring the future just stores up problems for later. There is no single correct state to live in because life is much more complex than that.

One of the biggest advantages of switching between perspectives is that it helps you get some distance. Remembering the past helps you see how far you've come, and reminds you of good friends and good times which have stayed with you and make you feel good now.

Looking to the future is a great way to deal with current problems, crises, disasters. Ask yourself how much this will matter in six

---

* Sorry, I spent too long living in Glastonbury – England's New Age capital.

months' time, or two years. Occasionally things go on mattering, but they're actually very few and far between. Dreams and plans are good too – they're what motivate you to keep going. So there's nothing wrong with the future.

The thing to avoid is becoming so focused on the past or the future that you miss what's going on now. It's like trying so hard to line up the perfect photo that you're separated from the action. The photo is supposed to be there to bring back memories, but in fact all you have is the photo and no other memory, because you weren't concentrating at the time. Don't do that with life. Notice it while it's happening. If you don't, you'll have wasted the time spent planning it when it was in the future, and you won't remember it when it becomes the past.

However, when there's down time, pauses for reflection, periods of analysis or contemplation, then you can look to the past and dream about the future, in order to give yourself a perspective on the present and keep your life in 3D.

RULE 83

Keep perspective

"Know what you want"

Some people seem to be born with an inbuilt sense of what they want and where they're going. If you're one of them, you can consider yourself very lucky. It's a great thing to have. But if you aren't one of those people, life doesn't come so easy when you're making choices about school, college, jobs, relationships.

It doesn't help that the people who do know what they want tend to think you should be like them. 'Come on!' they say, 'Have a plan!' The implication is that it's somehow your own fault that you have no driving ambition or sense of direction. Well, take it from me, it isn't your fault. And if the world was filled with people who all knew exactly what they wanted and how they were going to get it, I should imagine it would be a lot more cutthroat and aggressive than it is. So thank you for being you.

Nevertheless, the risk for you is that you'll just drift. It may not matter that much when you're in your early twenties, but by the time you're 40 you'll be frustrated and quite possibly a drain on other people if you're earning very little and slowly losing confidence as a result of feeling your life wafting past aimlessly. I've seen it happen and it's tough. So if you feel directionless when you're 20, address it now. Don't wait for the months to add up to years and then decades before you take action.

What action to take? First of all, make sure you're usefully employed doing anything rather than nothing. Even if you don't really enjoy your job, it beats being unemployed. That's because being unemployed saps your confidence, your self-respect and your bank account – which will make it even harder for you to find a sense of direction.

A significant majority of people who don't know what they want when they leave college sooner or later, a few years on, discover a direction that excites them. Think about what your passion is – even if you can't see a way to make a living from it, maybe there is one. You could work in a shop that sells your kind of computer games, or sports equipment, or artists' materials. You may not fancy the idea of being a shop assistant, but if it means spending all day with people who share your passion, perhaps you might feel differently? At least it will keep you busy while you find a better career.

Just keep trying new things, exploring new avenues. Consider going back to college, or retraining, or just trying something really different. If you stop looking and experimenting and meeting new people, I can guarantee you'll never find a job that inspires you. Don't panic and put yourself under pressure – you've got a job so you can take your time. But do position yourself to find out about new options and different jobs. Socially as well as professionally, stay alert and be ready to try anything. Your time will come.

RULE 84
You don't have to know what you want

"Guilt tells you where you're going wrong"

Guilt is a bad emotion, trust me. No, no . . . don't start feeling guilty about feeling guilty. I didn't say *you* were bad. I said *guilt* was a bad thing. Some people are overrun with it, almost always because of their upbringing: their religion, their parents, their teachers, some trauma in their past. And I appreciate that it's a very, very hard habit to shake. There's a comfort in it that, like any addiction, makes it hard to give up. But give it up you must, even if it takes you most of your life to do it.

I had a relative when I was younger who used to feel guilty about everything. She felt so guilty she had to talk to her friends for hours about what to do about it. None of which was any help at all to the people she felt she'd wronged, but at least it meant she could talk about herself and how she felt for hours. Because that's what guilt is about: you. It's a way of focusing on yourself that doesn't feel self-indulgent because you're shining a light on the shameful, dark parts of your psyche. Even so, it's sort of a back-handed compliment to yourself because the fact you feel guilty means you care, so you're basically a decent person.

Look, I'm not saying don't ever feel guilty. We all do. But guilt should be just a momentary flash of conscience that alerts you to the fact that you've messed up. It's what you do with the guilt that counts. You feel it (briefly), deal with it and then the guilt is gone. If you really can't deal with it, for whatever reason, then you need to drop the guilt anyway. Because it doesn't help anyone.

If you feel you've treated someone badly, or neglected them, or betrayed a secret, or let someone down, your guilt is in no way helping that person. It can't really, because you haven't got time to worry about them while you're so busy thinking about your own point of view.

I don't want to sound too harsh, because most people who are given to guilt have a complex relationship with it that goes back a long way, and the majority of them are truly not trying to be selfish. On the other hand, I do want to be harsh because – if this is you – you deserve better than to spend so much time berating yourself needlessly. You're damaging your self-esteem and your self-respect, and you need to understand what's going on so you can stop it. Because you really must stop it.

One reason why you must stop is because you need to start thinking about the person or people you think you've short-changed. Go and fix it, before you think about yourself. And then once you've fixed it, you won't need to think about yourself because it will all be OK again. You might *regret* what you did. Hopefully you'll learn from it. But you won't need to feel guilty.

One common factor among people who are prone to guilt is what petty things they feel guilty about. I remember my elderly relative spending hours fretting about the fact that she'd promised to visit a friend and then discovered she had a meeting so she couldn't make it. I couldn't understand why she didn't just phone the friend and say, 'Sorry, my mistake, I've double booked. How about Wednesday evening?' As an adult I now understand that she couldn't do that. Solving the problem would have deprived her of an excuse to feel guilty, and guilt can be so deliciously indulgent to wallow in, can't it?

RULE 85
Don't do guilt

"Someone will make it better"

When you're a kid and things go wrong, your mum or dad or some other relative does their best to sort it out, give you a hug, remind you you're doing OK, and get you back on your feet. If you didn't have this kind of family you've missed out badly, but at least you may have learnt to keep yourself going without outside help. Because good parents back off slowly as you get older anyway. They know that if they don't you'll never learn to get back on your feet after a knock.

And you do have to be able to get yourself back on your feet. Imagine you're physically injured and need to learn to walk again. The hospital fixes you up to a machine that supports your weight while you move your legs. That might sound good, but eventually you'll need to walk without the machine and you won't be able to unless you've learnt to support your own body. Other people holding you up is not the same thing as you taking your weight on your own two feet.

You'll take a few emotional knocks in life – we all do. If you're lucky, there will be friends and family on hand to help you recover. But in the end you have to do it for yourself. All they can do is give you a bit of back-up. And actually, once you realize you have to do it yourself, you realize that you don't need anyone else at all.

That's a much safer way to go through life, isn't it? Knowing that you can pick yourself up when you get knocked down. Friends and family are wonderful, but it's reassuring to know that while you might want their support, you don't actually need it.

It's a bit like giving up smoking (stay with me here . . .). Lots of people chew nicotine gum, smoke e-cigarettes or wear patches when they try to quit. The ones who succeed are the ones who recognize that the gum and the e-cigarettes and the patches are just there to make it a bit easier, they won't do your giving up for you. Only you can do that. Once you grasp that, you no longer need them.

So don't sit around waiting for someone else to make it all alright, or feeling that you're hard done by if you don't get support, or wishing your friends would give you a bit more help, or wondering why everyone else is letting you down. If you don't get back on your feet, the only one letting you down is you. It's tough, but it's true. The sooner you learn it, the sooner you can get back on your feet.

RULE 86

Pick yourself up (no one else will do it for you)

"Think through your problems"

How do you cope when you have a knotty problem to deal with? Most of us spin it around in our minds, looking at it from this side and that, considering all the possibilities, ramifications, alternatives, approaches and outcomes. It seems logical enough to keep thinking it through until you finally arrive – must surely arrive – at the best solution.

Except that sometimes you find the more you worry at the knot, the more tangled it gets. The problem becomes more complex under the microscope of your mind, and the solution gets further away from you. You end up more confused and frustrated, and the problem can start to obsess you. Should you take the job? Do you want to start a family? Is university for you? Is this really the right career path?

Thinking harder about things doesn't always make them better. Sometimes it makes them worse. It can be difficult to ignore the problem so you need to keep busy, fill your mind with other things, let the matter go for now. Counter-intuitively, this can actually get you closer to the answer you're looking for.

The subconscious mind is very powerful, and if you present it with a challenge and then go away and leave it alone, it will continue to puzzle at it without your conscious help. Often it will find you an answer, which it will feed back to you. Maybe it will give you some kind of inspiration, or a solution you hadn't considered, or perhaps just a gut feeling you can pick up on that tells you which way to go.

The sewing machine was invented by a man called Elias Howe. His knotty problem was working out how to get the needle to go through the fabric and pick up the thread from the other side. He spent years working on it. One day he fell asleep at his workbench, and he had a dream. He dreamt he was being pursued by cannibals carrying spears. When he woke up he realized that all the spears had holes in the points. That was his answer – he put the hole in the tip of the needle instead of the end where it is on a normal, manual needle. In his case a dream led to him becoming the second richest man in the USA.

I can't promise you such wealth and riches, but I can tell you that your subconscious mind often does a much better job than you of unravelling knots. And, as in Howe's case, it will notify you when it's arrived at an answer. So put your problem to it – in so many words if you like ('Hello subconscious, I've got a question for you . . .') – and then let it alone. Keep busy and see what happens.

RULE 87
Thinking hard doesn't always help

"Narrow down your options"

OK, I know I just said that it can help to stop worrying over a problem and just zen it. And I stand by that. However, that's not the only way to deal with every tricky problem. Sometimes you need to try something else before you get to that point, or after you've passed it.

One of my sons is coming up to choosing a university course. Or he might go straight to art school. There are a lot of options – and if he does choose university, he isn't sure which subject he'll study. There's an instinct in this situation to make a basic decision, such as art school versus uni, in order to contain the question and make it seem easier to cope with.

However, this is just the point at which you need to do the opposite. Look at *all* the options. Consider them all fully. When there's so much buzzing around in your head, you need some kind of gut feeling to tell you which way to go. You need to listen to your instincts. And the best way to do that is to think about all the paths you could take and then observe yourself thinking about them. Note your intuitive response to them.

This is a lot easier, and more informative, than drawing up long lists of pros and cons. And in the end these decisions are really down to instinct. Monitor how you react to each possibility. Are you unconsciously looking for excuses to decide against art school? Is there one subject at uni that makes you feel particularly excited, even if it's not the obvious one?

Look, if there was a clear best choice on paper, you'd know it. If there is, and you're still dithering, it's because deep down you don't like the obvious choice. You could spend days drawing up lists of pros and cons, and frantically trying to come up with more pros or more cons. Or you could recognize that that's what you're doing, and examine the reasons why.

Incidentally, I'm not a fan of weighing up pros and cons. Listing them is fine, to make sure you haven't missed any. But you can't balance them up, because they don't really weigh anything. I know that sounds facetious but what I mean is that you're not comparing like with like. There could be 50 reasons to do something and only one against, but it might be an absolute and overwhelming one. Maybe everything on paper points towards a particular course but it's far too expensive, or it's overseas and you would hate that. So by all means make sure you've thought of all the factors, and eliminate any options that prove to be unfeasible for some reason such as cost, but then listen to your gut feeling. That's the ultimate arbiter in any important decision.

RULE 88
Look at *all* the options

"Stick to a plan"

All through life you'll have people telling you that you need a plan. Everything needs a plan – big or small. So you need to plan how you'll get from A to B, a plan for getting all your bits of work in on time, a plan for getting qualifications you need to do X or Y, a plan for getting that perfect job, a plan for earning the extra money you need to buy a car – you get the idea.

And once you have a plan, the perceived wisdom goes, you have to stick to it. And that's where a lot of people come undone.

Truth is, life bowls googlies* at you every so often. And when that happens, your plan may well just go out of the window. The googlies can be good or bad, or indifferent, and sometimes you can't tell until years later which they were. Here are just a few possibilities that could happen to you:

- You fall passionately in love with someone who is desperate to live abroad.

- You're diagnosed with a serious illness.

- You're offered a wonderful job opportunity in a field you'd never considered.

- You or your partner become pregnant unexpectedly.

- Someone close dies suddenly.

- You go bankrupt.

- Your job becomes redundant due to new technologies.

Googlies throw your whole life up in the air, and there's no knowing where it will land. Yes, make plans, but do it in the knowledge

---

* Just in case you live somewhere where there's no cricket (perish the thought) a googly is a clever bit of bowling where the batsman expects the ball to go one way and it goes the other.

that you'll be lucky to get through life without some of them being totally disrupted. Or is that unlucky? A bit of unpredictability can be a good thing, and I know people who have been through some of the life-changing experiences above and looked back later to see how positive they were: serious illness, unplanned pregnancy, bankruptcy, redundancy – sometimes these things can herald a brave new life. You just don't know until it happens.

Sometimes, even without any of life's googlies, it's good to change things around a bit, be open to new possibilities, throw things up in the air. It doesn't do to get stuck in a rut. So always be prepared to be knocked off course – to go off map – whether the impetus comes from you or from an unexpected direction.

Whether the experience turns out to have been positive or negative, it will make you wonder why on earth you sweated so much over formulating and developing that perfect plan, when you find yourself somewhere totally different. I know someone who agonized over whether to go to university or drama school, and then ended up working in an African mission for 15 years because of a chance event.

RULE 89
Life is unpredictable

"Trust no one"

It's easy to advise you to go through life trusting no one, and I've met people who do it. They're invariably unsettled, anxious and always prepared for trouble. I generally find they're not hugely trustworthy either.

The thing is in life that people tend to get what they give. So if you're trustworthy, reliable, and show integrity, that's broadly what you'll get in return. That's assuming you don't choose to hang out with drugs barons and Mafiosi and underworld gangs – though some of them are probably trustworthy too. People would rather be good, and prefer to be liked. So they don't break trust without a reason. Of course it doesn't always work out like that, but that's pretty much everyone's intent.

If you don't give someone the chance to show they can be trusted, they'll be on their guard and resent your lack of faith in them. That makes them less likely to want to treat you well. So why not start out by expecting them to be reliable, and inviting them to live up to your expectations? Being trusted is a compliment, and one that people will appreciate and reciprocate.

Listen, you'll have the odd bad experience this way, I'm not denying that, but you'll have far fewer than if you go through life expecting people to let you down. Because that's just what they'll do.

You may not be aware of it, but you're the same. If people assume you're trustworthy, my guess is that you do your best not to disappoint them. Whereas if you sense that someone doesn't trust you, you feel no such compunction about letting them down. Sound familiar?

To go through life not trusting people is a miserable existence. You can never relax, you feel always disappointed and let down. The need to trust is not so much about whether the other person will or won't live up to it, but about what happens to you if you become the kind of person who can't trust others. Trust is a wonderful feeling, with all the love and security it brings, so why deny yourself? That way lies madness.

The joy you get when someone is trustworthy against the odds is worth being let down 100 times. I read a newspaper story about a man who befriended a homeless drifter, fed and clothed him, and eventually even gave him a job. How many of us could have shown that kind of trust? The guy lived up to it though, and got back on his feet. What a rewarding feeling that must have been for the generous bloke who invested in him. In the end, the only way to find out if someone is trustworthy is to try it and see.

RULE 90

Trust everyone

"Trust everyone"

Oh yes, I can contradict myself if I like. The fact is that you must be a trusting person in order to feel at ease with yourself and life. But there's no need to be stupid.

It's all about the stakes. How much does it matter if this person lets you down? Are you trusting them with a minor errand, or a major responsibility, or a big secret, or a sharp knife, or your life savings?

Everyone can be trusted to do some things. Your mum can be trusted to love you. Your boss can be trusted to tell you when you've messed up. A thief can be trusted to steal. When you come to put your trust in someone you need to weigh up how strong your confidence in them is, against how much it matters if they let you down.

So yes, trust everyone as a default setting, but know where the limit of that trust is. If you're dealing with someone you've known and loved all your life, you might trust them with a fair chunk of your money because they always repay you on time. Or you might not trust them because they want it for their new business and they have a history of bad investments.

You might, however, hand that same money over to a complete stranger . . . who is a qualified investment manager recommended by a close and trusted friend. You see? Trust, yes. But not blind trust.

I have one friend I can't ever trust to turn up on time for a social event. It's irritating. Then again, in a crisis I could count on him to step between me and danger without a second thought. Do I trust him? Yes . . . but it depends what for. So I invite him to parties after weighing up the likelihood of him letting me down about his arrival time (at least 99 per cent), against how much it will matter (very little).

I might come up with a different answer if I was weighing up whether to trust a stranger with my house keys, or a friend with a secret I really didn't want divulged, or my child to cross a busy road, or a colleague to fetch me a coffee. I'd consider what I knew of their track record, I'd think about how much a breach of trust would matter, I'd factor in a preference for trust over mistrust, and I'd see what answer came up.

Trust is a personal thing, and it has a lot to do with nuances and intuition about the person in question. Trust people to be who they are, not who you want them to be. I have friends I would trust with my life. But I wouldn't necessarily let them look after my cat.

RULE 91

Trust no one

"Sometimes you need a good moan"

You can moan to your parents, and to your partner and close friends so long as they can moan back to you. That's it. To other people, you present a cheerful face regardless of how you feel. You can mention negative things, but you can't whinge about them. Just grin and move on.

Why? Because moaning is habit forming, that's why. And because it's not endearing to listen to either. The more you get into the moaning groove, the more you'll do it. And that will bring you down, along with the people who have to listen to it.

Moany, whingy people are a pain. For one thing, it's fairly depressing to listen to. For another, they're usually talking about themselves so it's a pretty self-centred line of conversation. There's also the fact that the person on the receiving end may well have far worse problems, and they don't really need to listen to someone else's comparatively minor gripes. So moaners don't come across well or make themselves likeable.

If you get into the groove of looking for the negative, you can always find it. Allow your mind to dwell on the bad stuff and it will oblige. It will become increasingly adept at finding things to whinge about, and if there's nothing serious it will complain about the petty stuff. I've met plenty of Eeyore-ish characters who are never happier, it seems, than when they're depressing those around them.

Then again, I've met plenty of people whose lives are beset with all sorts of problems, but who are unremittingly cheerful. It makes them feel better – and goodness knows some of them need it. I've known cheerful paraplegics, positive cancer patients, one friend who is still looking on the bright side after the death of her son in a car accident. All of which goes to show that moaning isn't about your circumstances, it's about you. Think positive and you'll feel positive.

When someone asks how you are, don't say, 'Struggling on', or 'Mustn't grumble'. This kind of expression makes you feel as though life is an effort – yes, even if you think it's just an expression, it still influences your subconscious – and seems to invite people to ask you what's wrong (so you can have a moan). Tell people you feel great, and you really will feel a whole lot better.

Just a word about discussing bad stuff. You can tell someone about your awful journey to work this morning without moaning. Just give them the facts. Ideally turn it into a funny story as that will help you relax too. You can also pass on bad news when you need to. Your attitude and the words you choose will determine whether it's a moan or just a conversation. It's the way you tell 'em.

Now, as I've said before, the Rules in this book shouldn't necessarily be broken all the time, and you do sometimes need a good moan. Just restrict this to a small circle of friends and family and make sure that, apart from maybe your parents, they all reciprocate.

RULE 92

There are people who moan, and people who just get on with it

---

"Don't sacrifice yourself for a relationship"

I have one friend who has been fairly consistently single all his life. I think his longest relationship has been around six months. Perhaps I should put this into perspective by adding that he's in his late forties. When I've talked to him about it, he always says that he'd love to find the right person, but it would have to be a relationship for which he didn't have to make sacrifices to fit it into his life.

If you've reached your late forties without a serious relationship, I suppose you could think that made sense. I've certainly known lots of people who have held this view in their twenties and thirties. I've also known several survivors of unpleasant divorces who have taken refuge in this attitude.

However, if you're lucky enough to have – or ever to have had – a really strong relationship, you'll know that it doesn't work like that. Or rather, what these people like my friend are trying to avoid is actually compromise, but they can't tell it apart from sacrifice. So let's just clarify the difference.

Sacrifice is when you give up something without making any personal gain, especially when your partner doesn't reciprocate. That's unhealthy in a relationship, and no decent partner would knowingly ask you to do this.

Compromise is when both of you give up something or adapt in order to find a central position that you can both live with. Crucially, it leaves you better off personally than a failure to agree would do. That's because if it strengthens the relationship, and your partner is meeting you part way, then on balance you make a net gain. The trade-off is a beneficial one. You might both meet half way on something like how much money you spend on holidays, or you might balance up different concessions – one of you will do all the shopping if the other one does all the laundry.

A good relationship can't survive without compromise, not only because it's unrealistic to think that any two lives could mesh so exactly, but because it's the very fact that you are having to adapt to each other that seals your commitment. If the two of you are walking separate paths, that's not actually a relationship. You might as well just walk away from each other – you wouldn't notice the difference. It's the interweaving that creates the bond. That's not to say that all compromises are worthwhile, or that every relationship that entails compromise will succeed. But no relationship, however strong its potential, can thrive without compromise.

RULE 93

It's the compromises that make relationships worth having

"Feelings should be rational"

I can remember saying as a child that I was upset, or angry, or disappointed, or hurt. Often I would be told, 'That doesn't make sense . . .', followed by an explanation of why my feelings weren't rational and therefore – by implication – weren't valid. Maybe it 'made no sense' to be hurt by what someone said when they hadn't meant it that way, or it wasn't 'logical' to be angry when a situation was of my own making.

If anyone has ever told you anything like this, I can reassure you now that they are wrong. Your feelings are what they are. Right and wrong don't come into it. That's what makes them feelings and not thoughts. Rational thought is right or wrong, logical argument is right or wrong, but feelings are just that: feelings.

We have feelings we want and feelings we don't want. Feelings we can shout about and feelings we shouldn't express. Feelings we enjoy and feelings we don't. Feelings we share and feelings we keep to ourselves. None of these feelings is wrong or invalid, even though voicing them may not always be appropriate.

It's true that you can change your feelings – your emotional reactions – over time. But you need to accept your mind's natural response first before you can start to adapt it. It's no good telling yourself that you shouldn't feel this or you mustn't feel that. Of course you can, and then if you don't like the feeling you can work to change it.

I've known people admit to feelings they felt dreadful about – having a favourite child, for example, or disliking someone who had only ever been kind to them. Well, clearly these aren't feelings to be acted on, or even openly talked about, but they are still valid. Only by recognizing them can you hope to address them and eventually change them.

If anyone tells you that you have no right to feel angry, or you shouldn't be upset, or there's no sense in feeling regretful, or you ought to feel grateful, or you mustn't feel hurt, you have my full permission* to ignore them completely (but politely). You feel what you feel. In fact, if you start the sentence 'I feel . . .' and are interrupted by the word 'But . . .' it almost always means the other person is about to try to invalidate your feelings. The best response is to repeat firmly, 'I *feel* . . .'

Feelings aren't bad. If you don't like a feeling you can try to change it, but don't feel guilty about it. The problem with people suggesting that your feelings should be rational is the implication that you can control them. That in turn implies that you are to blame if you have feelings that you 'shouldn't'. Not so. You can control whether you express them, and in what way, but you're not responsible for your instinctive emotional responses.

RULE 94

Feelings aren't right or wrong – they just are

---

* Not that it's worth anything, but it might help. Ideally give permission to yourself.

"Eat, drink and be merry . . ."

There's nothing wrong with enjoying yourself, and I'm certainly not one to advocate abstention when it comes to food and drink. But the Rule above ends '. . . for tomorrow we die'. While there's no denying that we'll all end up dead eventually, there's no need to hurry it along. So by all means be merry, but don't be as foolhardy as the Rule implies.

It's hard to believe that you're mortal when you're young. As life goes on, people start to fall by the wayside and sooner or later – if you're not one of them – you realize how fine a thread you hang by until the Fates decide to cut it. Life is more fragile than it seems, and death is devastating to those who are close. Until you have experienced this at first hand it's hard to encompass, but some grief lasts forever and ruins lives. And all too often it's caused by the briefest and most unthinking of actions.

I knew a lad who climbed into a car with a friend who had drunk too much. He was a great guy – never drank when he was driving, but for some crazy reason he let someone else do it and then drive him home. Except he never got there. I expect he'd done it loads of times before and always got away with it. And that's the big mistake. You think because it's always been OK before, it will be OK this time. But actually the more times it's been OK before, the more chances are silently running out for you.

The lad's mum had an RIP tattoo done on the back of her neck after he died, dedicated to him. A couple of months later, she was talking to another young man about not driving too fast. He said he knew he should slow down, but somehow he didn't. So she showed him her tattoo and said, 'When you get home, have a look at your own mum, and think about where you think she should have her tattoo done when you die'.

We owe it to our mums, dads, brothers, sisters, children, friends and everyone around us to do our best to stay alive. Our lives aren't only our own, we share them with the people we love, and we have a responsibility to them to be sensible about driving, drinking, drugs, safe sex, dangerous sports, crime and anything else that could threaten us. I'm not saying you shouldn't learn to skydive if you want to, but take safety seriously. It doesn't make you a scaredy-cat, it just means you're responsible and you care about the people close to you. If you die because you can't be bothered to look after your own safety, how angry do you think that will make the people who love you most? And with good reason. Looking after yourself is one of the best ways you can look after them.

RULE 95
Stay alive

"I want doesn't get"

Now there's an expression I heard a lot as a child, and I still hear other parents using it when I'm out and about. I have never understood it, even when I was young. You tell your parents what you want and they say 'I want doesn't get', and they don't give it to you. So next time you want something you carefully avoid mentioning the fact, and they don't give it to you. As far as I could see as a child, nothing got you what you wanted.

Well, maybe as a kid you're in a lose/lose situation. As an adult, however, 'I want' is the only thing that does get you anywhere. Regardless of your conditioning as a child, you need to learn to be clear and specific about what you want. If you can't explain what you want, how can you expect anyone to give it to you? Whether it's in a relationship or at work, with friends and family or talking to the bank, you absolutely have to be able to state what you want.

Of course you'll ask for things that are reasonable, and you'll ask politely. There's no need to demand with menaces, or to expect to be given things without question or compromise. Good manners should prevail at all times, because you're a decent person, and because the alternative is less likely to work.

What on earth was it supposed to mean? I suspect that in a more polite age it meant you shouldn't start a sentence with 'I want . . .' but with 'Please may I . . .', and is a matter of simple manners. Even so, it's actually much clearer for other people to hear you state what you actually want when it matters.

If you want a pay rise, for example, you'll never get it unless you ask. And if you ask deferentially, in a 'Please may I' tone, it implies you're asking a favour, which you're not. You're saying, politely, 'I believe I'm worth more than I'm being paid, and I want a pay rise that reflects that'. Obviously you'll have to justify this, but assuming you can, you have every right to lay your cards on the table in this way. It shows that it's a fair exchange – your labour for their money.

In a relationship, if you need to discuss problems you should of course do it with respect and consideration. You can still help your partner if you can state, for example, 'I want us each to be responsible for our own laundry', or 'I want to go out for a meal together at least once a week'. It makes it much easier for you both to see what criteria you must fit your solution around.

So be polite and friendly at all times, as always, but for goodness' sake say if you want something. How else can anyone tell you if it's OK to have it?

RULE 96
Ask for what you want

"If it ain't broke, don't fix it"

I suppose this applies to a few things in life, such as cupboard doors and biscuits. But most things of any complexity that ain't broke at least need maintaining, or they pretty soon will be. Your car may run nicely, but you have to look after it if you want it still to be going in a year or two.

If your life ain't broke, that doesn't mean you can just chug along aimlessly, waiting for the next pothole to trip you up. Which is exactly what it will do if you don't look where you're going. It may be fun when you're 20, but by 40 you'll wonder why you haven't made it any further down the road.

You have to look up, look ahead, keep setting yourself targets and dreams and ambitions and objectives. Good enough isn't good enough. You can do better than that. As soon as your life starts getting too comfortable, shake things up a bit. Don't wait for it to break before you fix it. Find some new stimulation to energize you, some kind of challenge that keeps you excited.

Otherwise you'll get bored. And it's easy to go on being bored in a comfortable, ain't broke kind of way, until you realize that years have slipped by and you've achieved nothing. What are you going to leave behind when you're gone? A comfortable stagnation, like a cosy cushion no one sits on any more? Is that honestly good enough for you? It shouldn't be. Life is a wonderful, exciting, thrilling, fascinating privilege, and if we're lucky enough to be here, we should make an effort to prove that existence worthwhile.

Find your own way to justify your existence – whatever works for you. I don't care if you save stray dogs or produce wonderful artworks, pass on an old skill or go into politics, help the sick or design a garden. Just keep looking for ways to repay the gift of being allowed to be here for a lifetime. Show Fate or the gods or whoever you believe in that life isn't being wasted on you, that you're making good use of your time.

When it comes to your life I'd say that 'If it ain't broke, don't fix it' is about as defeatist as you can get. And we Rules players certainly aren't defeatists. We roar and shout and make our voice heard – somewhere, by someone who will appreciate it. So let's hear no more of this silly, idle, leave-things-as-they-are talk. If it ain't broke, that's a great starting point for improving it.

RULE 97
Look up

"Find yourself a safe job"

I'm not sure there is such a thing as a safe job any more. Nevertheless, some jobs are safer than others. The world will always need accountants and sales people and civil servants – or at least for a good few decades yet. And for some people, numbers are a fascination and accountancy really appeals, or selling just fits their sense of competition and interest in people.

Suppose, however, your real passion is winter sports, or films, or wild animals. A lot of people (most of them older than you) will tell you that you'll never get a steady job as a tobogganist or an actor or a wildlife photographer. They'll urge you to choose a career where you can find a job with relative ease, which you can stay in for a long time. Your dream, they'll tell you, is impractical and unrealistic and you'll never get a decent job – or if you do, it won't last.

Many people view any form of freelancing or self-employment as inherently too risky, and they'll advise you to get yourself on someone else's payroll so you're more secure.

My observation, however, is that while this works very well for people who long to be retailers or nurses or teachers, it just doesn't work for people who don't. A few years down the line you won't feel safe and secure and relieved you didn't become an astronaut. You'll spend your life frustrated and feeling hemmed in and trapped in a job you increasingly resent for being the opposite of what you wanted. It may be that you already are some years down the line, and feeling just that way.

On the other hand, I've never met anyone who regretted having followed their passion. Even when it didn't work out, or they worked it out of their system after a few years and moved on, they've always seemed happy and fulfilled. Yes, even if they had much less money and job security than they could have had.

Like anything else, you have to work at following your dream. There may not be many people who make it as rock stars, acrobats, explorers, MPs or pyrotechnicians, but some do, and you could be one of them. If you put enough work into finding out what it takes and then making sure you fit the bill, why not give it a go? What's the worst that can happen?

Listen, even if you end up in a job that doesn't inspire you, you'll be far more content if you tried for your dream job and didn't make it than if you never tried.

RULE 98
Follow your passion

"Protect your property"

My grandmother had a fabulous collection of outfits which she'd collected throughout a lifetime of travelling and working in theatres. When she got older, she stuffed them all in a trunk and when we visited as children we'd use them for dressing up. Some of them were, frankly, far too good for this, as my mother often used to point out – while we were busy ruining them. My grandmother always waved her away, saying, 'Darling, I don't care. People are more important than things'.

On the face of it, this is so obvious it hardly seems worth mentioning. However, it's frighteningly easy to forget it when your own property is at stake. I'm still not sure if my grandmother was right about the costumes (as teenagers we'd have loved some of those outfits, if only we hadn't been allowed to trash them years earlier), but I've frequently seen people worry so much about property it gets in the way of relationships.

Some people would rather fall out with a neighbour than concede them one inch of land, or a section of fence, that might well belong to the neighbour anyway. I know other people who won't lend perfectly replaceable items in case they get damaged, despite the damage this might cause to the relationship with the person wanting to borrow them. I had a relative who hardly ever visited when we were kids because she was too worried about what might happen to her house when she was away. And I know countless people in whose houses I can never really relax for fear I'll leave a fingerprint or squish their carefully plumped cushions.

Most of the time, there's no conflict between people and things, and you can enjoy both. But it's easy to get sucked into the kind of materialism that puts property first, without even noticing you're doing it. Then when conflicts like the examples I've just given do arise, you can get your priorities the wrong way round.

Look, please feel free to own as much as you like and can afford, but make sure that you don't allow it to control you. Keep it firmly in its place, give it a good talking to, and don't let it get uppity. It's just stuff. Very nice stuff maybe, but still only stuff. Whereas people . . . well, everyone is irreplaceable. If you lost everything material that you owned, but kept your family and friends, you'd be fine. But the other way around?

This Rule is especially useful when it comes to those objects of sentimental value that were given to you by special people, or remind you of someone you love. Maybe even someone who has died. Of course you treasure them, but remember that they only have value because of the person they represent. The person themselves – or your memories of them – are far more important. So if you lose that ring, or break that ornament, or tear that photo, it's not the end of the world. After all, it's only a thing.

RULE 99
People are more important than things

"You can't change horses in midstream"

This expression is mad. Of course you can change horses in midstream. Every case is different, but often it's the most sensible option. Lots of traditional rules contradict each other, and this one contradicts the principle that 'if you know you're in a hole, stop digging', which I find much more helpful.

If you're midstream on a horse that is clearly not going to make it to the other side, why wouldn't you change? When your life, or any part of it, is heading for disaster – or even just heading somewhere you don't want to go – my advice is to change direction as soon as possible. There's always some way you can get things back on track.

I've known people leave school or uni before the end of their course, or hand in their notice and embark on an entirely new career, or get out of a flagging relationship before it gets any more serious, and in many, many cases they've clearly been making the right decision.

I will say that changing horses in midstream is rarely the *easiest* option. But that just means that almost no one does it without a good reason. Why would you choose the harder option if you didn't have to? If, despite being tougher, you're convinced that this is the right route for you, then go ahead and make the change. Good luck to you, and well done for having the courage to leave the beaten path.

Not only can you change course if something better presents itself, you can also change if you realize you're treading a dark and dangerous path and you need to get out. Sometimes in life we lose our way and fall into bad habits, or fall in with a bad crowd. But it's OK, because you're allowed to change horses in midstream. You can always find a new white charger and head for the light.

I sometimes hear from readers who want to know what to do when they discover they've already spent their lives breaking Rules. Listen, even Rules players break Rules every day. We try not to, but sometimes things don't go to plan. It's OK – the trick is to start every day afresh.

It's not a religion – the Rules are just guidelines for a happier, more successful life. There are no broken Rules that can't be fixed just by changing what you do from now on. And don't beat yourself up if you don't live up to your own standards first time, every time. Cut yourself some slack, but don't stop trying.

RULE 100
It's never too late to start following the real Rules

RULES TO FOLLOW

I wouldn't want you to think that I'm advocating some kind of rebellious rule-breaking extravaganza for the sake of it. No, I've got to be honest here – there are some things routinely trotted out by parents, teachers and well-meaning friends that *will* stand you in very good stead. The tricky bit is spotting them.

There's no point in breaking Rules for the sake of it, you know, however satisfying it might feel.* There's far more satisfaction to be had from following Rules, if they make sense. What Rules players become really good at, over time, is developing a well-tuned radar capable of quickly evaluating little nuggets of advice, and swiftly deciding which to break and which to follow. But it does take time, so to help calibrate your inner radar, here's where I flag up some of these bits of gold dust, so you can quickly pick them out from the chaff.

I've put together ten top Rules which are worth following. I've never seen anyone go far wrong following these particular principles, and you can trust them to serve you well.

---

* Or is that just me?

No man is an island

Usually trotted out when someone is cutting themselves off from others, and possibly cutting off their nose to spite their face in the process. It's quite right too. All of our lives interlink with others, whether we like it or not. Every action we make – or decline to make – affects other people, and other people's actions affect us. This isn't something to moan about when others are getting in our way or getting on our nerves. It's just how life is. What's more, it can be a whole lot easier to achieve big stuff if we have others on our side.

The only reasonable response to the connected nature of life is to embrace it. We are connected to everyone, whether they're friends or colleagues or family who we see regularly, or strangers on the other side of the world who we only hear about. So never separate an act or decision of yours from its consequences. There's no such thing as 'collateral damage'. All damage should be factored in from the start.

Social media has made this Rule truer than ever. It gives us a way of seeing the link we always had to each other far more clearly. You can strike up friendships now with people in Singapore or Peru or Iceland who you've never met. You can also troll people in Singapore or Peru or Iceland – except of course that Rules players never troll anyone, because they understand this Rule.

Every significant choice you make – beyond trivia such as whether or not to have a cup of tea, or what to watch on TV – will affect someone else, and you need to be aware of the effect it will have and take responsibility for it. If you post something abusive on social media, that's not just a name or a comment you're responding to. That's a real person. OK, so it's a real person who you happen to disagree with, but it's still someone with passions and feelings, and who knows what back story? You don't know how they arrived at their beliefs, what their challenges in life are, but you do know that your post will have an effect.

Even when you've put your phone down or switched off your computer, you'll still make decisions at work and at home that will have ramifications like ripples in a pond for other people. Not only can you not avoid this, it's all part of what makes being human so wonderful. Yes, even though it undoubtedly makes some decisions far harder. On balance, it would be mad to cut ourselves off from other people because we'd lose so much more than the short-term benefits we might gain.

I can't express this Rule better than its original author, one of the greatest writers of all time – John Donne. If you've not encountered him before, he was writing in the seventeenth century, which is great news because it means I can quote him without my publishers having to pay lots of money for the privilege. So I shall. He wrote this meditation during an epidemic of potentially fatal sickness, which he himself had contracted, and heard the bells tolling for another death:

> No man is an island, entire of itself; every man is a piece of the continent, a part of the main. If a clod be washed away by the sea, Europe is the less, as well as if a promontory were, as well as if a manor of thy friend's or of thine own were. Any man's death diminishes me, because I am involved in mankind; and therefore never send to know for whom the bell tolls; it tolls for thee. (*No Man is an Island, Meditation XVII*)

> **NOT ONLY CAN YOU NOT AVOID THIS, IT'S ALL PART OF WHAT MAKES BEING HUMAN SO WONDERFUL**

Two wrongs don't make a right*

Why would anyone think that two wrongs would make a right? Well, generally because they consider their own action to be justified by the wrong done to them, and therefore they don't see it as a wrong. Or rather, they choose not to see it as a wrong. Deep down they usually know that it is.

It's very natural when someone does something that hurts or upsets or angers or embarrasses you, to want to respond in kind. It's human nature. But that doesn't make it right. And it certainly doesn't resolve anything. In fact, it generally escalates hostilities and you can end up with dozens of wrongs on both sides, which still don't make a single right.

I remember at the age of about 3 smacking another child in my class. He wouldn't get off the rocking horse, as I recall, and I knew the teacher would have smacked him if she'd been there. She wasn't, so I did it for her. He called her over and told her. I was expecting thanks but, to my surprise and horror, her response was to smack *me*.

I can still remember my total bafflement. Either it was OK to smack people or it wasn't, surely? I simply couldn't see what I'd done wrong. I now understand why smacking has been outlawed in UK schools, and should be everywhere. If it's wrong (which it is), then it's wrong. And by doing the same wrong to me the teacher wasn't putting things right, she was making them worse. My child's eye logic could see this perfectly clearly.

---

* Although three rights do make a left. And a negative × a negative is a positive. But that's different.

If your neighbour lops off half your tree that overhangs their garden without checking, that's wrong. However, if you respond by blocking their car from moving by parking your own in front of it, that's wrong too. You've just made everything worse, and stooped to their level, and effectively given them free rein to play their music loudly late into the night. On so many levels, you've made the wrong choice, and lost the moral high ground.

The smallest wrongs right up to the biggest just compound each other. It applies to petty squabbles with colleagues or family, right up to international level, as history shows, if you go looking for examples. It's the reason why you shouldn't retaliate when your sibling gives you an apple-pie bed, and it's why capital punishment is wrong.

> ## THE SMALLEST WRONGS
> ## RIGHT UP TO THE BIGGEST
> ## JUST COMPOUND
> ## EACH OTHER

When in Rome, do as the Romans

I've been to funerals (bit of a morose example, but stay with me) where everyone dressed in bright colours and danced and let off fireworks. I've also been to funerals where everyone wore black and spoke quietly. I wouldn't dream – and nor would you – of wearing garish clothing to the second kind of funeral. That would be disrespectful. But nor would I wear black to the first one.

What is sometimes less obvious is that this same respect should follow in other more everyday situations. The way you behave at work, the language you use in front of different friends or family (especially if you're ever given to swearing), the level of noise you make on the beach or at a party, the procedures you follow when dealing with your local council or your university.

This is about fitting in and not causing offence or disruption. And while it is a matter of respect, it's not only that. It's also far more productive for you to act as if you belong, even if it requires effort. People will accept you more readily, and therefore be more inclined to give you what you want – co-operation, help, support, attention, respect.

A friend of mine went on a train journey that took her across the border from Thailand into Malaysia. It was on a rural railway, not used by tourists. The two countries are adjacent but with very different cultures of course. The friend struck up conversation with a young, cool looking Malaysian guy after crossing the border. As they chatted, the topic of cultural differences arose, and the man confessed that he did find her shorts and vest top a bit disrespectful. He suggested politely that in order to get the most from every interaction in Malaysia (and especially off the tourist route) longer shorts and a more classic T-shirt might be a real asset.

Look, I know that some systems, organizations, procedures, dress codes, protocols, house rules are plain daft. At least to some of us. Why should it matter what you wear or how you address people or who speaks first or what paperwork gets filled out? Often it really doesn't matter what the rules are, but it still matters that you follow them. Yes, even if they're bonkers. It's not about the rules, it's about the fact that everyone is part of them. If you buck the system, you're effectively putting two fingers up to it, and that's plain rude. If you really hate it that much, go and work somewhere else or find other friends or join a different club. But don't engage with a system and then not co-operate with it.

I'm not saying that there's no room for protest. Obviously if you feel strongly that an approach is unethical or wrong you can say so. One option is to do this from outside the system, but there are times when you take a stand within a company or group that you're part of. Even so, you can campaign for a thing without actually doing the thing – you can lobby for flexi-hours at work while working 9 to 5. Generally speaking, if you flout the system openly, you undermine your own campaign by creating animosity unnecessarily.

> ## IT REALLY DOESN'T MATTER WHAT THE RULES ARE, BUT IT STILL MATTERS THAT YOU FOLLOW THEM

Don't judge a book by its cover

Many years ago now, when I was in my early twenties, the boss I was working for left. He was replaced by a new boss, Mike, who I just couldn't get on with. He wasn't good at the job either, as far as I could see. After a few weeks I went to his line manager and complained that I couldn't work with him. At which point I discovered that he'd already been to say exactly the same thing about me. The line manager hauled us both in and banged our heads together,* quite rightly. And Mike and I ended up agreeing to start again from scratch.

I have to say, to Mike's credit, that he really did start over, and so did I. And you know what? It turned out that he was a lovely guy, with a great sense of humour. I was right that he wasn't good at some parts of the job, but he was brilliant at others. And he had no ego about the stuff he wasn't good at – he used to say to me, 'You'd better deal with that. You're much better at it than I am'. Eventually we both left the company, but we kept very much in touch and remained close friends.

I learnt a huge amount from that episode. I'd nearly lost myself a dear friend simply by thinking that Mike was the unco-operative waste of space I'd first assumed. And several times since then I've given people I didn't warm to a second chance. Often I find I've been wrong and, you know what, even if that's not the case there's never anything to lose by sticking with them for a while to see if they have hidden depths.

I have a distant relative who is an extremely bright man, and built a little business empire before selling it and retiring. As they say in Derbyshire (where he's from), 'He's worth a bob or two'. You

---

* Metaphorically, of course. I wasn't born in the Dark Ages.

wouldn't know it to look at him though. His clothes are tatty, his hair is wild and unkempt. I've witnessed people in upmarket shops or restaurants treat him as if he must be mentally ill, or an alcoholic or have something unspecified 'wrong with him'. In fact, he just doesn't place any importance on attire, appearance or possessions. Which is, frankly, pretty refreshing.

Yes, some books are very much what the cover promised, but you should never assume it. That's why this is a Rule always to follow, even if the plot does occasionally turn out to be as thin as you suspected, and the characters as weak. The Rule is always to leaf through the pages to see if maybe the cover isn't a true reflection of the contents.

It's not simply that you could be wrong. That you might be mis-judging someone. That they might have more to offer than you thought. It's also about what you're missing out on if you don't look beyond the cover, just as I'd never have had Mike's friendship if I hadn't been made to reconsider my initial judgement.

And it's about your attitude to people in general. I've found through life that when I've treated people I didn't take to as if they were worth my time, I've had a far better response from them than I otherwise would. If I raise my expectations of other people, they respond far better to me than if I don't. That means I get more co-operation, make more friends and so on. If I give people second chances, I'm giving myself a second chance too.

> # IF I RAISE MY EXPECTATIONS OF OTHER PEOPLE, THEY RESPOND FAR BETTER TO ME THAN IF I DON'T

RULE 5

For every action there is an equal and opposite reaction

Newton's third law of motion of course. But also a Rule of inter-action with other people. If you push against someone, they'll push back. You can't blame them, they're just following a natural law. One of the most obvious examples of this is between parents and teenagers. The more resistance a parent shows to their child becoming independent, the harder that child will rebel. But that's far from being the only example.

This partly explains why some people fall into the 'two wrongs don't make a right' trap. It doesn't justify it, mind, but it helps explain it. The fact is that if someone pushes you, your instinct is to push back. It's human nature as much as it's a law of nature. It can take effort to resist it – which is what you have to do, as we saw in Rule 2.

Taking it a step beyond that Rule, it also means that if you push against someone else, you have to take responsibility for the fact that they'll push back. If you attack, they'll go on the defensive. Which means that it's your job as a Rules player to make sure that you don't push people because you'll always create a situation that is harder to resolve than the one you started with – the one that made you want to push. You've increased the other person's resistance. Introduced more friction. OK, enough with the phys-ics metaphors, but the reason we use the same words to describe these human interactions that the scientists use to describe natural laws is precisely because this Rule holds true in both worlds.

Do you know what a non-Newtonian liquid is? It's one which behaves as a liquid if you move it gently, but as a solid if you hit it with force. The best example is custard made using cornflour.

If you fill a swimming pool with custard you can swim through it smoothly. But if you stamp on it, the force of your feet hitting it makes it respond as a solid, so you can actually run across it as if it were a road. Stop moving and you'll start to sink into it as a liquid.

It's a great analogy for the best way to deal with people who disagree with you. Always aim for agreement rather than conflict. Tackle them gently and carefully and you'll be able to work smoothly through the problem. But use force and they'll present you with a metaphorical brick wall.

Of course, there's a positive side to this Rule too, as I hope you've realized. If you give to other people, they'll give back to you. Maybe not straightaway, but if you go through life being as generous as you can, you'll find that your opinion of human nature is much higher because people will respond in kind.

> ## IF YOU PUSH AGAINST SOMEONE, THEY'LL PUSH BACK

There's no such thing as a free lunch

Back in the nineteenth century, a lot of US saloon bars would offer free lunches. Sometimes these could be decent meals, but of course you'd want a drink with your food, maybe two . . . and the drinks weren't free. The fact is that there's always a catch, and while extreme cynicism may not be an ideal quality, a bit of healthy scepticism is never a bad thing. And most of all when the thing you're being offered looks too good to be true. Because it probably is.

Any commercial organization is in it to make profits. And even if you can't see how they're making money out of you, in a normal transaction they will be. They're offering you a free prize draw in order to capture your data to sell, or that bargain is only there to draw you into the store. BOGOF (buy one get one free) deals aren't really giving you an item for free. They're selling you two items at half price, and they're doing it because you might not buy even one of them otherwise.

Insurance companies have worked out that on balance you'll pay them more in premiums than they'll give back in payouts. That's how they stay in business. (And it's why it's not worth insuring anything unless either it's a legal requirement, or you couldn't afford to replace it if it breaks down.) If the company wants you to do something, it's because they know that in the end it will mean they can take more money off you than if you don't do it.

And what about your employers, offering you inducements, perks, compassionate leave and all the rest of it? They expect increased loyalty and commitment and hard work from you in return. They're not really saints.

It's true of most personal transactions too. Maybe not with your closest family and friends – although philosophers might argue that they still want love/approval/gratitude or something similar in return. But an offer of help is often seen by the other person as a down payment for some kind of favour from you in return.

Of course, sometimes these offers are worth taking up. Sometimes the BOGOF is a bonus for you because that item was actually on your shopping list already. So I'm not saying you shouldn't ever accept anything that looks free. I'm just saying that it isn't actually free, so you need to work out what the real cost is, and then decide whether it's still worth it. Keep your eyes open, and always question what the catch is. Look at it from the other person's or company's point of view and work out what's in it for them. Don't be naïve or you'll be exploited. Be street smart and understand the true nature of every transaction, so you can make a proper choice.

> KEEP YOUR EYES OPEN,
> AND ALWAYS QUESTION
> WHAT THE CATCH IS

Do as you would be done by

I can remember being told this as a child and it made me cringe, I think because it was always said in a deeply sanctimonious voice, and it always accompanied some kind of misbehaviour on my part. Nevertheless, now I'm older and I've seen a bit more of life, I can't deny that it's exactly what the Rules are all about. That is to say that people who follow it are happier than those who don't.

We know we want to be decent, good, kind people. Sometimes we get overcome with emotion and it's hard to see what the right way to behave is. This Rule is a reminder that actually it's very simple. If the roles were reversed, how would you like to be treated? There – that's your answer. That's how you should handle other people in any tricky situation.

Of course, you have to be honest. It's no good pretending to yourself that you'd expect to be treated badly if you'd behaved in the way the other person has to you. The question is, how would you *like* to be treated? And the answer is always with politeness and respect.

Part of this is about being a good person. Part of it is about maintaining the moral high ground (see Rule 94 from *The Rules of Life* for more on this). And part of it is about encouraging people to treat you well. It's not just what we *should* do, it's also that people mirror our behaviour. So if you always speak and act respectfully, you'll be responded to in kind. OK, maybe not every time, but certainly most of the time.

And finally, it's about earning the right to respect for yourself. If you want to be treated well yourself, you have a responsibility to respect other people, look after them, see their viewpoint, be supportive, look for solutions to problems that work for both of you. If you can't do that, you have no moral right to expect the same behaviour in response. This is why, even if some people refuse to return your courtesy, you have to keep on proffering it.

This doesn't only apply to conflict, mind you. It also applies to smiling at shop assistants, thanking people who are helpful, tipping waiters, letting other cars in at busy junctions, and helping little old ladies across the road. In fact, the more you go through life treating other people as you'd like to be treated, the easier it becomes to default to it naturally.

IF YOU WANT TO BE TREATED
WELL YOURSELF, YOU HAVE
A RESPONSIBILITY TO
RESPECT OTHER PEOPLE

RULE 8

The pen is mightier than the sword

This sounds like a very old-fashioned saying, but that's because I'm using the Rule in its traditional form. It's all about how you get your point across when you want to argue, persuade, convince, debate, or otherwise impress something on someone.

The old-fashioned phrasing needs to be taken with a pinch of salt, but its meaning is sound. It might be better to say, 'Words are better than aggression'. Doesn't sound as catchy, does it? However, it indicates that the words can be either written or spoken. And I'm glad to say we don't generally resolve our arguments these days with swords, but the message is that words beat any form of aggression, from insults to physical violence.

I hope that as a Rules player you don't need telling that violence isn't acceptable (except in extreme circumstances in self-defence or defending others from attack). However, this Rule isn't just about not hitting or attacking other people, it's also about not threatening to do so, and not being abusive in your words or your manner.

Obviously I'm going to tell you that these things aren't Rules behaviour, because they're not. However, that's not the only reason to follow this Rule. As with all the Rules in this book, it's about what actually works in the long run. And the fact is that abuse and violence won't succeed in the way that words will.

Whether you need to write a letter, or prepare something to say face to face, if you want to win an argument you need to have the strongest case, not just the strongest right hook. Arguments are won with words. If you resort to other measures your best hope is to bludgeon the other person into silence. If you achieve this, and get your own way, you still haven't actually won the argument. You've simply silenced the opposition.

If you genuinely have the better case, you need to make it clear by putting together a coherent argument and winning people over to your way of thinking. You can't be sure you're right unless you know why and, if you know why, you can explain those reasons to other people. If you feel you're not good with words, find someone who is and get them to help you find a few choice phrases or persuasive examples or clinching arguments to express yourself with. Then get people on your side with logic and empathy. And remember that if you're not asking them to lose, to back down, to admit defeat, they're far more likely to agree with you. Try to make them feel as if you're both on the same side so they have nothing to lose by agreeing with you.

And if that doesn't work, consider the possibility that maybe the other person actually has a better case than you . . .

> ## IF YOU GENUINELY HAVE THE BETTER CASE, YOU NEED TO MAKE IT CLEAR BY PUTTING TOGETHER A COHERENT ARGUMENT

RULE 9

Keep dry, and away from children

A friend of mine saw this exhortation on a box of matches, and immediately adopted it as a motto for life. However, I'm using it here metaphorically. There's nothing wrong with getting wet (there's no such thing as bad weather, just the wrong clothes) and somebody has to go near children.

On a matchbox, this directive is stating the glaringly obvious. Assuming you know how to use a match (which they must be assuming, as there are no instructions) you will be well aware that they won't work if they're wet, and that it's not really a great idea to hand them over to a 4-year-old.

Nevertheless, while it seems quite unnecessary to tell match users to keep the matches dry, it's surprising how often we miss the obvious. I know a man who cannot drink more than one glass of alcohol without becoming miserable, and then – if he keeps drinking – aggressive. He's not an alcoholic, and will go weeks without a drink until the next social event comes along, where-upon he has three or four glasses of wine or a couple of beers, and feels depressed and does things he regrets later. You would have thought that it would be glaringly obvious that he should stop drinking after the first glass (or maybe not even start?) but he seems unwilling to adopt this manifestly sensible policy.

A friend of mine always gets into relationships with women who are neurotic wrecks. It never works, because the women in ques-tion aren't currently in a state to have a successful relationship, and he always ends up broken-hearted. He is well aware of this tendency and yet every time he introduces his friends to a new girlfriend – surprise, surprise – she's lovely but just like all the others. Clearly something in him is drawn to needy women, but since he knows what the problem is you'd think he'd listen to his own advice and steer clear of the women at the neediest end of the spectrum.

Ah yes, he should follow his own advice. You frequently know perfectly well that you're breaking your own rules, doing something you know can only turn out badly, and yet you persist. Why? Bloody-mindedness? Excessive optimism? Not wanting to listen to advice you don't like, even when it's coming from you?

Sometimes, as with the matches, the glaringly obvious needs stating. If you know you have a particular weakness or susceptibility, tell yourself in so many words – out loud if it helps – and heed your own advice. Consciously resolve on your way to a party not to start drinking, or back off when you first meet yet another attractive but needy woman and tell yourself out loud to wait until she's ready for a relationship before you think about making a move.

Look, you know where your vulnerabilities lie. Whether it's the thing you always say that you know will set off a row with your partner, or sticking your head in the sand about things you wish weren't happening at work but are and need dealing with. Just learn to tell yourself the glaringly obvious a bit more often. And then listen to yourself.

> # SOMETIMES THE GLARINGLY OBVIOUS NEEDS STATING

Give it time

Sometimes things go really wrong. Horribly, miserably, catastroph-ically wrong. When you go through a break-up or a bereavement or a natural disaster or a redundancy or some other traumatic event, it can be hard to see past the next few days or weeks. Often your mind struggles to cope with what has happened, and if the event was unexpected you might be in emotional shock for months.

Platitudes and clichés aren't helpful at times like this, and it can be tempting to react angrily to anyone who tries to tell you that 'time is a great healer'. You don't want to hear it from other people because it suggests they're trying to make you look ahead before you're ready to, and therefore they don't really understand what you're going through.

Nevertheless, I can get away with saying it because you can't shout at me (not so I can hear anyway). And you can say it to yourself. Not because it's time to 'move on' (whatever that ghastly expres-sion means) but because it helps to give you some perspective.

There *will* come a time when you'll be OK with the fact that your parent died, or you were bullied, or you lost your job, or you got divorced. You may never be happy about it, but it will become integrated into you eventually. I can look back on dreadful events in my past – we all can – which I now accept as being part of myself. They're what make me the incredible person I am today. And it's the fact that I'm looking back on them from a distance that makes them alright. Not great necessarily, not always happy memories, but OK. I can even say that a few things that were truly dreadful at the time are honestly absolutely fine now, and I can see how I gained from them in the long run.

A lot of the key to adjusting to these traumatic changes is to understand that what used to be normal has gone, and there will be a new normal. Yes, whether you like it or not. And you may well not like it. You may fight it tooth and nail. But there will come a day when you will wake up and not notice the difference because it has stopped being different. This is how it is now.

So I guess the Rule here is, when you're going through those deeply difficult experiences, imagine yourself looking back on them in two, five, ten years. That will help you to see that this miserable state isn't going to last forever, however much it might feel like that now. Even though there will always be a sadness when you look back, you will be able to choose when you look back. And once you've found a new normal, it will bring with it new happiness and new enthusiasm and new zest for life.

> ## WHAT USED TO BE NORMAL HAS GONE, AND THERE WILL BE A NEW NORMAL

Take your whole life to another level with the complete Rules of Richard Templar

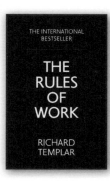
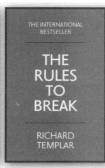
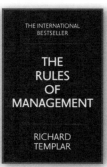
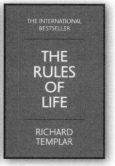
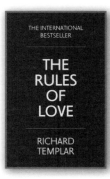
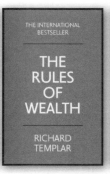
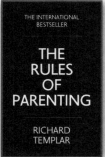

You'll get older but not necessarily wiser

There is an assumption that as we get older we will get wiser; not true I'm afraid. The rule is we carry on being just as daft, still making plenty of mistakes. It's just that we make new ones, different ones. We do learn from experience and may not make the same mistakes again, but there is a whole new pickle jar of fresh ones just lying in wait for us to trip up and fall into. The secret is to accept this and not to beat yourself up when you do make new ones. The Rule really is: be kind to yourself when you do muck things up. Be forgiving and accept that it's all part of that growing older but no wiser routine.

Looking back, we can always see the mistakes we made, but we fail to see the ones looming up. Wisdom isn't about not making mistakes, but about learning to escape afterwards with our dignity and sanity intact.

When we are young, ageing seems to be something that happens to, well, old people. But it does happen to us all and we have no choice but to embrace it and roll with it. Whatever we do and whoever we are, the fact is we are going to get older. And this ageing process does seem to speed up as we get older.

You can look at it this way – the older you get, the more areas you've covered to make mistakes in. There will always be new areas of experience where we have no guidelines and where we'll handle things badly, overreact, get it wrong. And the more flexible we are, the more adventurous, the more life-embracing, then the more new avenues there will be to explore – and make mistakes in of course.

As long as we look back and see where we went wrong and resolve not to repeat such mistakes, there is little else we need to do. Remember that any Rules that apply to you also apply to everyone else around you. They are all getting older too. And not any wiser particularly. Once you accept this, you'll be more forgiving and kinder towards yourself and others.

Finally, yes, time does heal and things do get better as you get older. After all, the more mistakes you've made, the less likely that you'll come up with new ones. The best thing is that if you get a lot of your mistakes over and done with early on in life, there will be less to learn the hard way later on. And that's what youth is all about, a chance to make all the mistakes you can and get them out of the way.

WISDOM ISN'T ABOUT NOT MAKING MISTAKES BUT ABOUT LEARNING TO ESCAPE AFTERWARDS WITH OUR DIGNITY AND SANITY INTACT